Developing an Interdisciplinary Science of Organizations

✳ ✳ ✳ ✳ ✳ ✳ ✳ ✳ ✳ ✳ ✳ ✳ ✳ ✳ ✳ ✳ ✳ ✳ ✳

Karlene H. Roberts
Charles L. Hulin &
Denise M. Rousseau

❋ ❋ ❋ ❋ ❋ ❋ ❋ ❋ ❋ ❋ ❋ ❋ ❋ ❋ ❋ ❋

Developing an Interdisciplinary Science of Organizations

✱ ✱ ✱ ✱ ✱ ✱ ✱ ✱ ✱ ✱ ✱ ✱ ✱ ✱ ✱ ✱ ✱ ✱

Jossey-Bass Publishers
San Francisco · Washington · London · 1978

DEVELOPING AN INTERDISCIPLINARY SCIENCE
OF ORGANIZATIONS
    by Karlene H. Roberts, Charles L. Hulin, and Denise M. Rousseau

The Jossey-Bass Social and
Behavioral Science Series

Special Advisor,
Methodology of Social and
Behavioral Research
DONALD W. FISKE
University of Chicago

To Edwin Ghisell
mentor, friend, and source of inspiration

Preface

This book is an attempt to define the content and limits of an area of interest commonly called "organizational behavior" or "organizational science" and to discuss what organizational science is as reflected in empirical research and theory development. We apply the concept of paradigm to organizational disciplines and discuss four paradigms around which organizational research and theory tend to cluster. We also attempt to develop a common language consisting of a small number of concepts useful to individuals who are interested in human behavior in organizations. Using this language, we propose a framework to guide the development of one's research or theoretical work (or at least to put it in perspective with regard to the field as a whole) and to evaluate empirical and theoretical contributions of others. We then focus on a problem that emerges frequently in the organizational sciences but is usually ignored, the problem of aggregation. Finally, we provide examples of past research to which our framework might be applied with profit and discuss some policy implications of viewing research and theory development in the organizational sciences in the way we recommend.

Developing an Interdisciplinary Science of Organizations is intended for a diverse audience, including researchers and practitioners from different backgrounds who are concerned with producing and using research about individuals in organizations. Members of this audience often have very little in common in terms of disciplinary background—well-trained researchers from one discipline will view as obvious points unfamiliar to researchers from other fields—but they do have common interests in analyzing and understanding organizational phenomena.

This is not a "how to" book: it does not tell how to compute a covariance matrix or a mean, nor does it describe procedures for randomly allocating subjects to experimental and control groups. The material here is philosophical in the sense that we are oriented toward basic concepts and their interactions, not toward operationalizations and manipulations. Had this been a medical book, we would not have discussed how and where to make an incision to remove a diseased appendix. We would have written instead about skeletal, nervous, circulatory, and digestive systems and how a knowledge of these systems and their interactions is necessary to research and practice in medicine.

All three of us were trained as classical, industrial psychologists. Our biases were originally consistent with those of our mentors who stressed the ubiquity of the influences of individual differences on responses. We now contend, however, that individual differences are not the entire story—or even its most interesting part. It is apparent that we are discouraged with the present state and directions of organizational research and theory development. We have tried to shed our original biases and to the degree that we have done so our success has been purchased with considerable effort. We hope to provide here a blueprint that can be used to help researchers, theoreticians, and practitioners broaden considerations of sources of influence on responses made by people in organizations—and, coextensively, our research.

Despite our own backgrounds as psychologists, we hope that what we say here is of interest to organizational researchers, theorists, and practitioners who work in other disciplines. We do not want to argue that all organizational research and theory development is psychology or sociology or systems research. Organizational science is fast becoming recognized as a discipline in its own right despite continuing arguments about whether it is a science at all. It is by nature not a coherent, homogeneous, consistent approach to understanding a related set of phenomena. This lack of coherence probably reflects both the complexity of the phenomena we study and the divergent backgrounds of those of us who call ourselves organizational scientists. We believe that people from a wide range of disciplines can make contributions to our understanding. But we are concerned with the lack of integration of research findings, research efforts, and theory development in the field. In fact, we have not before seen a serious attempt to discuss simultaneously viewpoints emanating from various disciplines and their possible integration. It is to these problems that we address the bulk of our remarks.

Whether our framework represents a radical departure from past practice and suggests substantial revisions of existing paradigms is left for the reader to judge. If we only suggest minor alterations in standard, accepted research procedures, then we are more timid than our analysis of the situation suggests we should be. A number of points raised and issues discussed may appear obvious. Perhaps they are. If they are, we should see numerous examples of research and theory development following from consideration of them. We do not. We cannot determine whether the reason is that the points are difficult to implement in research practice, that they suggest research strategies that generate results difficult to interpret, or that they have been implicity considered by researchers and rejected. We think that the issues we raise are not obvious and that working with them should help us all sharpen our thinking about doing and interpreting research and about generating theories. If the issues have been considered and rejected, we should see any number of explicit statements about why they were rejected. We do not.

This book began as two separate methodological papers by Roberts and Hulin presented at a symposium of an annual meeting of the American Psychological Association. Following that symposium, Bert T. King of the Office of Naval Research suggested developing a technical report that discussed the kind of research we would like to see done in organizational science. Edwin Ghiselli, to whom this book is dedicated, urged us to expand the material from the report into a book. Some time later, we met Donald W. Fiske, who has been a source of encouragement to us ever since. Throughout the writing of the present book, we benefited greatly from conversations and correspondence with Fiske, who served as a source of ideas and an evaluator of materials. His influence has clearly changed the material over the years of its writing. Those who know him as an iconoclast in personality research and theory may not recall his early association with research concerned with responses people make in complex organizations and environments, and they may be surprised at his involvement in a book on organizational research and theory.

During the 1976–77 academic year, Rousseau designed and conducted research using a framework similar to that discussed here, a framework intended to integrate research results and theoretical discussions across different levels of observation in organizations. We became acquainted with her work; and, after Rousseau read some of our earlier materials, we persuaded her to assist us in completing the book.

A number of persons, through their work, made substantial contributions to our thinking about organizational research without realizing it: D. Campbell on science and knowing, W. Mischel on situational characteristics and constraints, B. Ekehammar on situation/person interactionism, J. K. Galbraith on interdependencies, A. Kaplan on theory, L. Zadeh on fuzzy concepts, J. Thompson on organizing, and J. Conant on understanding science. We have attempted to acknowledge our intellectual indebtedness to them where appropriate.

Roberts and Hulin are indebted to the Office of Naval Research, which supported us in this and other work. The University of California at Berkeley and the University of Illinois at Urbana-Champaign provided sabbatical leaves to begin the book. The James McKeen Cattell Foundation and the Center for Advanced Study at the University of Illinois furnished sabbatical supplementary funds for us both. Fred E. Fiedler made available an office and desks in his laboratory at the University of Washington during a part of our sabbatical leaves. H. Peter Dachler, William Glick, Terence Mitchell, Charles O'Reilly, Jeffrey Pfeffer, and James Terborg took time from their busy schedules to comment on manuscript drafts for us. To all of these people, we extend our sincerest thanks.

August 1978

KARLENE H. ROBERTS
Berkeley, California

CHARLES L. HULIN
Champaign, Illinois

DENISE M. ROUSSEAU
Ann Arbor, Michigan

Contents

The Authors

✳ ✳ ✳ ✳ ✳ ✳ ✳ ✳ ✳ ✳ ✳ ✳ ✳ ✳ ✳ ✳ ✳ ✳ ✳ ✳

KARLENE H. ROBERTS is professor of business administration and research psychologist at the Institute of Industrial Relations at the University of California at Berkeley. She received her B.A. degree in psychology from Stanford University in 1959 and her Ph.D. degree in psychology from the University of California at Berkeley in 1967.

Roberts is a fellow in the American Psychological Association (APA) and a member of the Academy of Management. She was chairman of the Scientific Affairs Committee Division of Industrial/Organizational Psychology of the APA. She has been on editorial boards of *Journal of Vocational Behavior, Journal of Applied Psychology, Journal of the Academy of Management,* and *Organizational Behavior and Human Performance.* Roberts received a James McKeen Cahell Postdoctoral Award given by the American Psychological Association and an IBM Postdoctoral Fellowship in International Business. Her major research interests are in organizational communication, the impact of variable work week schedules on responses to work, and substantive and methodological questions of cross-national organizational research.

CHARLES L. HULIN is professor of psychology in the College of Liberal Arts and Sciences and in the Institute of Labor and Industrial Relations at the University of Illinois at Urbana-Champaign. He was graduated from Northwestern University with a B.A. degree in psychology in 1958. He received his M.A. degree from Cornell University in 1960 in labor relations and his Ph.D. degree in psychology from Cornell University in 1963.

Hulin is a fellow in the APA and is a member of the Academy of Management. He served as chairman of the Scientific Affairs Committee of the Division of Industrial/Organizational Psychology of the APA. He is currently associate editor of the *Journal of Applied Psychology* and is on the editorial board of *Organizational Behavior and Human Performance.* At the University of Illinois at Urbana-Champaign, Hulin has served as an associate member of the Center for Advanced Study during 1975–76 and as associate department head of the psychology department from 1973 to 1975. His research interests focus on the study of environmental, organizational, and individual characteristics and their impact on responses of individuals in organizations.

DENISE M. ROUSSEAU is an assistant professor of psychology at the University of Michigan and a study director at the Institute for Social Research there. She earned her A.B. degree in psychology and anthropology in 1973 and her M.A. degree (1975) and Ph.D. degree (1977) in psychology, all from the University of California at Berkeley.

Rousseau is a member of the Academy of Management, the American Psychological Association, and the American Sociological Association. Her primary research interests are in organizational technology and the relationship of work to nonwork.

Developing an Interdisciplinary Science of Organizations

✻ ✻ ✻ ✻ ✻ ✻ ✻ ✻ ✻ ✻ ✻ ✻ ✻ ✻ ✻ ✻ ✻ ✻

CHAPTER 1

✳ ✳ ✳ ✳ ✳ ✳ ✳

Diversity in Organizational Research and Theory

✳ ✳ ✳ ✳ ✳ ✳ ✳ ✳ ✳ ✳ ✳ ✳ ✳

What is organizational science? What should it be? Why is it important to develop a science of organizations? A major difficulty in
answering the first of these questions lies in the nearly impossible
task of obtaining consensus about what an organization is.

What is an organization? Consider the question as an em-
piricist might. Ask ten friends or colleagues to define an organization. Ask them to specify the boundaries of an organization, to
indicate what is included and what is excluded. Ask them to define
connections among subunits in organizations and to tell you what
characteristics are essential for an object to be classified as an or-

1

ganization. One outcome of this exercise will be that there is little consensus about what constitutes an organization.

Despite this lack of consensus, our purpose here is to discuss organizational science as we think it is and as we think it should be. We hope that out of this discussion an answer to the third question will emerge. Before addressing these overall problems, we need to place them in some perspective by considering in this chapter the following issues: Why are some people interested in studying organizations? What is possible to understand about organizations, and where do we get our information about them? What kinds of things are investigated in the study of organizations? How do we know when we have learned something about organizations? What similarities and differences exist between those who engage in organizational science and those engaged in other scientific endeavors?

Why Study Organizations?

Why do we study organizations? One answer is that we are interested in organizations simply because they are large and important environments in which we exist and respond and which we adapt to in varying degrees or leave. The study of organizations reflects an interest in environmental influences on responses. This is one reason, but it is not the only reason. The increasing pervasiveness and importance of organizations make it necessary to understand how people are influenced by and, in turn, influence them. Population growth and relative affluence have resulted in an organizational population explosion. This factor and others contribute to the growing influence of organizations on our lives. All of us are members of multiple organizations and are influenced by activities in organizations of which we are not members.

As an example of the growing importance of organizations, consider the evolution of service organizations. During early stages of the westward movement in this country, the family—or at most a small group of families—carried out most functions now entrusted to collections of individuals we call organizations. Health care, defense against common enemies, schooling, food production and preparation, dispute adjudication, manufacture of household goods, entertainment, care and protection of the aged, and even care and support of those unwilling or unable to care for themselves were functions assumed by family members.

When the nation's economy developed to the point at which families were able to live above a subsistence level, it was feasible and more efficient to entrust many of these activities to loose organizations of specialists. These early organizations existed solely to assist families. Early educational systems, for example, consisted of individual teachers loosely connected with one another, under the direct supervision of families whose children they helped educate. Many defense systems consisted of ad hoc groups of people who assumed responsibility for upholding laws and punishing wrongdoers.

Members of early organizations had exactly as much authority as the families in their communities allowed them. However, it became increasingly tempting for people to abdicate more and more power and control to organizational members. Abdication enabled people to substitute money for time and energy and left them free to engage in more pleasurable pursuits. The result was gradual increase in the authority, autonomy, and power assumed by members of interlocking systems or organizations.

Another reason for the study of organizations is that it has practical value. Most of us work in organizations. Knowledge about how our individual activities fit into the total scheme of those organizations is helpful if we are to survive. Using this kind of knowledge, we might be able to change our responses to one or another feature of our workplaces to obtain a better fit between ourselves and our organizations. At least we could know something about the kinds of problems we might face at work. This idea has been adopted in a programmed text on leadership training (Fiedler, Chemers, and Mahar, 1976). Rather than following the usual approach of trying to change leaders' behavior or personalities, Fiedler trains leaders to recognize situations in which they are likely to fail. The leaders are then taught either to avoid such situations or to try to change their environments to make them resemble situations in which they are likely to succeed. Early results of this kind of situational engineering are promising. As parts of our environments, organizations constrain responses that occur to them. Thus to understand how environments in general, and organizations in particular, constrain what people do, exhaustive investigations of mechanisms by which environmental and organizational characteristics are generally translated into responses are essential.

Closely related to this last point is that we need to learn as much as we can about how organizational characteristics *specifically* relate to responses. The study of these relations considers the totality of characteristics of an organization as a potentially important set of predictors of responses, no better or worse than (until shown to be so) any other set of predictors. Unfortunately, the potential influences of organizational characteristics on a broad set of responses remain generally unstudied. At the same time, we need to know how individual responses influence characteristics of organizations.

Yet another reason for studying organizations is the interdependence of organizations and individuals; organizations themselves are interdependent. As Pfeffer and Salancik (1978, p. 40) state, "Interdependence is why nothing comes out the way one wants it to." No doubt, this is often frustrating to organizational participants. Pfeffer and Salancik (1978, p. 40) offer an example of interdependence: "Any event that depends on more than a single causal agent is an outcome based on interdependent agents. Interdependence is the reason you cannot find the word in the *American Heritage Dictionary*—an outcome which depends both on your obtaining the dictionary and looking up the word and on the publishers' having included the word in the volume." That organizations are interdependent is illustrated when we question something we usually take for granted—for example, that General Motors designs its automobiles. As Pfeffer and Salancik (p. 32) ask, *does* General Motors design automobiles? To what degree is automobile design in General Motors dependent on things done in the Environmental Protection Agency, the Department of Transportation, various consumer groups, and other organizations?

As interrelationships and interdependencies among organizations become increasingly pervasive, members of those organizations often feel impotent to the point of despair. Such individuals should be interested in learning the mechanisms through which interactions of individuals representing different organizations influence other people. Thus, in our attempts to learn what influences our lives and how, and in our attempts to restructure these multiple influences, we draw information from organizational science.

When we take an even broader perspective of organizations, it is increasingly apparent that various interrelationships among different organizations affect variables and responses conceptually and operationally many steps removed from them. For example, a decision made by members of the Organization of Petroleum Exporting Countries in 1973 is expected to eventually drive the price of technologically sophisticated equipment high enough that it will become economical to replace equipment with labor. In the long run, one result should be higher employment rates in the United States. At the same time, the new jobs are expected to be relatively undesirable to many people by reason of repetitiveness, wages, promotional opportunities, and so on. Thus, a decision made in Geneva in 1973 may eventually result in more—albeit perhaps undesirable—jobs for United States workers. Depending on the undesirability of the new jobs and on other factors, the long-term employment increase may also result in increased turnover in the even longer run.

As we have noted, organizational decision makers have pervasive influence on members of the organizations and possibly even on members of other organizations, and organizational characteristics, policies, and standard operating procedures likewise have great influence on people. In turn, people respond to those influences—possibly by changing organizations. These points are illustrated by noting that if the air traffic controllers at O'Hare International Airport in Chicago decided to follow to the letter of the law the enforcement of allowable intervals between incoming flights, the resulting slowdown would be felt throughout the airline system in the United States and even in air travel in other countries. Within hours, planes as far away as Paris or Tokyo would be delayed in their takeoffs. Airline performance would be slowed significantly. As another example, recall the immediate effects of the 1973 decision by members of OPEC on the lives of people throughout the industrialized world. The existence of such pervasive organizational influences is reason enough to devote resources to studying organizations.

What Can We Learn—and How?

What is possible to understand about organizations, and where we do we get our information about them? To avoid engaging in debate about whether we are discussing a science, a research area, or an accumulation of half-truths, we assume that just as there are sciences of physical objects and sciences of social phenomena, there can be a science of organizations. In defining what a particular area of study is, it is often more important to say what it is not. This disclaimer is of concern to everyone interested in human behavior in organizations. It is important that there be a clear understanding of what is in the archives in the field and what might be added. We all need to know what is and what is not within the grasp of the seeker. *Organizational science should not attempt to understand and explain organizations or individuals in organizations.* Such endeavors are beyond our abilities. It is impossible at this time to understand even one individual. Wigner (1964, p. 995) stated in his Nobel laureate address: "Physics does not endeavor to explain nature . . . it only endeavors to explain the regularities in the behavior of objects. . . . In fact, the specification of the explainable may have been the greatest discovery of physics so far." A similar discovery by organizational scientists might prove equally enlightening.

We can and should try to observe, quantify, and explain regularities in responses of individuals and groups in organizational contexts. By *regularities* we do not mean there must be a one-to-one correspondence between a stimulus and a response or between two responses. We simply mean that response A frequently occurs after stimulus B, or that it frequently occurs in situation C, or that responses X_1 and X_2 occur together far more often than chance would indicate. In fact, if a given response *always* follows a given stimulus, the connection generates little scientific interest. Skinner (1938) notes that only because eating *sometimes* follows the presentation of food do we bother to postulate a need state called "hunger." The lines differentiating randomness, regularities, and certainties are not clearly drawn, but their general locations determine our areas of interest and our research concentrations (see Chapter Three). We should try to explain regularities in responses of organization members. Some researchers try to explain regularities in global responses or responses assessed directly at the organizational level. Other researchers are interested in regularities in aggregated responses—those assessed at one level and grouped to reflect something about a more abstract or general level. Thus, individual responses are collected to reflect some aspect of work groups, departments, organizations, and collections of organizations (see Chapter Two). Observation of regularities of responses and the situations in which the regularities occur is the elementary aspect of organizational science. The extent to which we can cause response regularities to occur by manipulating situations and can generalize from particular observations, making predictions about unobserved (and perhaps unobservable) constructs and processes, is a frequent subsequent step for researchers and theorists. Finally, we might become more interested in trying to observe and explain irregularities and absences of consistencies in responses.

Astronomers, for example, do not attempt to "explain" the universe. They study events occurring in it. They initially observed and attempted to explain regularities in orbits of observable planetary bodies. After observing striking regularities in orbits, some astronomers became interested in observed *irregularities* in the orbits of some of these planetary bodies. The observed deviations from expected paths led them to postulate the existence of unobserved planetary bodies that influenced what could be observed.

A similar example comes from the literature on schizophrenia in monozygotic twins. A general finding is that monzygotic twins have a high concordance rate for schizophrenia: if one twin is found to be schizophrenic, the other is likely to be. This high concordance is the empirical basis for a genetic explanation of schizophrenia. Recently, however, the study of monozygotic twins discordant with respect to schizophrenia has occupied more attention in efforts to understand the etiology of the disorder. It is even suggested that the study of female monozygotic twins discordant for schizophrenia will prove more valuable than the study of discordant male twins, because the expected base rate of concordance among female twins is higher. The point is that these irregularities would provide little information were it not for the base rate of regularities which have been observed and established (Wahl, 1976) and against which irregularities can be compared.

Relevant to the issues of studying observed irregularities to learn more about regularities and studying regularities to understand irregularities are the questions of whether one should study normality by studying deviance and whether one should study deviance to understand normality. We tentatively answer "yes" to both questions. However, whether we are yet in a position to study irregularities in organizationally relevant responses is a troublesome question. We probably have not yet sufficiently established regularities as backgrounds against which response irregularities in organizations can be assessed. An even more serious question concerns organizations which have been studied intensively and which have provided our basic data. It is entirely possible that organizations to which we have access are deviant and irregular. Decision makers in healthy, expanding, profit-making organizations may be reluctant to donate resources generously so that an organizational scientist can obtain data to test a hypothesis that may be of no use to the particular organization. Hence, what we observe consistently and think represents normality may in fact be some blend of deviance and normality.

Organizational scientists show a rather striking lack of consensus about what constitutes "proper" organizational research or theory development, the major issues and questions, and "proper" methods of answering these questions. This problem will be explored in detail in Chapter Two. The lack of consensus should not necessarily be regarded as evidence that organizational science is doomed. It is probably more an indication of the relative youth, diversity, and vigor of the field. Only after an area of social science has been a topic of investigation for a number of years and after pet and set paradigms have been developed (and perhaps after senescence has set in) would we find striking agreement about what constitutes the area and who belongs to it. Despite the lack of consensus, what we have in common is where we look for interesting phenomena in organizations (real or simulated). Let us consider what content of interest is similar and dissimilar across organizational scientists.

What Do We Study in Organizations?

The responses that organizational scientists look at—whether responses by individuals or aggregated responses by members of groups—are few, compared with the totality of responses made in organizations. Rarely do we care, for example, how many times a manager blinks his or her eyes in a day. We look for responses that define organizations in terms of enduring patterns of social interactions. We therefore select for study measures reflecting the relative productivity or effectiveness of individuals, groups, or organizations. We usually select for observation responses thought relevant to the efficient attainment of organizational goals consistent with high quality of work life for organizational members.

Hence, organizational scientists begin by focusing on sets of interesting (to them) outcomes. An example is structure, which is an outcome of things people do to realize their goals. Productivity and effectiveness of individuals, groups, and organizations are thought to be important organizational outcomes. Job satisfaction, coalition formation, decision making, power distribution, tendencies to leave or change situations, and even some physiological responses, such as those thought related to stress, are among the dozens of responses interesting to organizational researchers.

There is much less agreement among us about what characteristics are antecedents to or predictors of major sets of responses or outcomes. Researchers in this field will explain the same set of responses in as many ways as the researchers have backgrounds. The range of explanations is quite broad. Despite our common interest in a relatively narrow and homogeneous set of responses, our intellectual *Weltanschauungen,* environments, and histories determine what abstract concepts we invoke to explain observed consistencies in responses. They also influence the way we attempt to examine the validity of our concepts.

Consider the example of turnover in the United States labor force. An economist might explain trends in turnover levels by reference to national economic conditions. A political scientist might invoke the concept of alienation of working classes due to efforts by the Establishment to maintain power while denying power to other groups. A sociologist might talk about a conflict between work values of lower socioeconomic classes, or perhaps of younger workers, and work values held by supervisors and by people who design organizations. A psychologist would probably introduce job dissatisfaction as the cause of turnover. It is entirely likely that all these explanations are basically correct. In fact, they may even reflect the same underlying process—that process supposedly leading to turnover. The following analysis shows how they might do so.

It is possible that during times of economic expansion and growth, workers compare their status with that of others and feel deprived by comparison. This relative deprivation might be more severe among workers from lower socioeconomic groups. During such periods, the Establishment, as represented by employing organizations, solidifies its power by a process of expansion. Perceptions by younger workers that this happens can easily lead to their changing work values—placing greater emphasis on leisure time and money than on hard work, high-quality performance, and dedication to an organization. These changes place younger workers in conflict with older supervisors. All these trends might result in increased job dissatisfaction among some segments of the working population, particularly among the young. Increased job dissatisfaction, combined with the ready availability of job alternatives, should increase turnover. Thus, not only may the four explanations of the same response tendency be compatible, they may depend on the same underlying unobserved construct.

If our example is realistic, a major problem is that, given the current state of the study of organizations, we may never learn whether these four explanations are basically the same. There is no common language for discussing the underlying predisposition for individuals to leave their jobs and no agreed-upon framework for integrating observed regularities across levels of aggregation of individuals and associating them with constructs. Constructs from different levels of abstraction and analysis (national economic trends, alienation among members of socioeconomic classes, and individual affective states) are invoked to explain individual decisions to leave jobs aggregated to several levels (turnover among individuals, in work groups, in organizations, and in the national labor force). We cannot emphasize too much that, without integration across several levels of analysis, organizational science will remain distressingly noncumulative.

How Do We Know We Have Learned Something?

How do we learn about complex phenomena in our scientific or everyday world? More important, can we specify the process of knowledge acquisition and know when we have learned something? Learning might be characterized as blind trial and error, accompanied by selective retention of information that seems to lead to desired outcomes (Campbell, 1960). In spite of appeals to cognitions and thought processes as essential, learning may not be notably different from taking a random walk and retaining for future use the reinforced choices at each of the choice points. The process of acquisition of scientific knowledge at this stage in the development of our research area might be similarly characterized. Large numbers of people (researchers) are busily engaged in throwing material at a wall. That which sticks is defined as mud and is seen as reinforcing the wall. That which falls off is something else and should be discarded. Our early experiences floundering around in organizations might be no different. No one researcher or scientist knows enough about organizations in general to plot our wanderings and compare them with the optimal path. There are also very few people who know any one organization well enough to guide us from the building directory in the lobby (or from the organizational chart) to an appropriate decision maker without our entering at least one blind alley.

With these limitations, how can we decrease the randomness in our research, and how do we learn something that will help us explain regularities and consistencies of responses in organizations? Almost all the data making up the body of facts and knowledge commonly agreed to define organizational science are relations among sets of characteristics, among sets of responses, and—less frequently—between sets of characteristics, on the one hand, and sets of responses, on the other. These are normally relations between variables taken two at a time. For example, we have seen too many studies relating age to job satisfaction, sex to job satisfaction, or race to job satisfaction. The excess of such studies indicates one of our problems: Job stress, perceived role ambiguity, decision making, organizational growth, or any other responses do not occur in isolation from one another. Nor do various antecedents of these responses occur independently. Hence, it is probably necessary to summarize the influences of a number of antecedents acting simultaneously on a number of responses.

Most of our information about organizations and their members comes from the kind of bivariate relations just described. Reliance on large numbers of bivariate relations would not necessarily be a shortcoming if the many relations could be integrated into nomological networks. These networks, each containing multiple links among antecedents and responses of interest, would then form the basis for selecting additional observations for organizational scientists to describe and interpret. We know we have learned something when the multiple links have been established and are interpreted logically.

For example, studies of job turnover have established two kinds of bivariate relations—those between job characteristics and turnover and between employee characteristics and turnover. We have learned that a number of job characteristics are related to a high frequency of decisions to terminate employment; incumbents in jobs with these characteristics are more likely to quit than incumbents in other jobs in the same organization. Low wages, little or no formal training, dirty working conditions, noise and noxious odors in the environment—all these contribute to job leaving. We also know that characteristics of job incumbents are related to turnover decisions. People who have little education, who have histories of "job hopping," who have few family responsibilities, who are young, or who have had wages garnisheed are more likely to quit their jobs than other employees. Attempts must be made to integrate these two sets of relations with turnover into statements about underlying dimensions of jobs and workers and their interrelations that predict termination decisions.

Occasionally we do see empirically established links among the multiple antecedents of a response as well as between each antecedent and the response. Less frequently these links are accompanied by links among multiple assessments of the response. The networks established are usually impoverished, as regards both the number and the strengths of the connections among observations. In addition, these relatively impoverished networks are used to contribute to the development of even more abstract concepts and explanatory models.

Have we learned anything about organizations from the kind of network building and model development we usually see? Yes, but less than we sometimes think. We have learned that variation in a particular set of characteristics is accompanied by variation in another set of characteristics (or responses). For example, multiple hierarchical levels and extreme functional specialization in organizations are accompanied by information distortion. Outside threats lead to increased loyalty to either organizational subsystems or suprasystems, depending on a number of factors. In other words, we can make statements like "When X_1 is present, X_2 is also regularly and predictably present; when Y_1 occurs, Y_2 also occurs more often than chance." We have learned little about constructs underlying such observations, although we are willing to go beyond our data and make inferences about these underlying constructs. Nonetheless, when we can make verifiable and valid statements like those above, we have learned something about organizations. Progress beyond this point calls for greater refinement of networks of variables. We need to develop richly articulated networks, each of which is concerned with an important problem. By *richly articulated* we mean that there must be empirically established relations among variables in the networks and that these relations must be free of experimental or measurement error.

These activities are the initial steps in developing nomological networks. Nomological networks are the interlocking systems of laws that constitute theories (Cronbach and Meehl, 1955). The laws in nomological networks may relate observable properties to one another, theoretical constructs to observables, or theoretical constructs to one another. For a construct to be scientifically admissible, it must occur in a nomological network in which at least some of the laws involve observables.

We learn more about any theoretical construct through elaborating the nomological network in which it occurs. We elaborate a network by making its components more definite. Adding a construct or a relation to theory is appropriate if it generates networks that are confirmed by observations or if it reduces the number of nomologicals required to predict those observations. The refinement of networks also occurs when their constructs predict the absence of relations one does not see.

After the initial development of a network composed of theoretical constructs and observed variables, a verbal or mathematical definition of what is meant by the entire network of relations must be provided. This definition should lead to the definition of new and testable relations between more concrete and more abstract or general concepts. (Alternatively, a next step may be to study narrow manifestations of concepts and their relations to other variables and concepts in attempts at greater precision.) Concepts or variables that lead to hypotheses confirmed by new data and contribute to our understanding of other regularities in behavior in organizations should be retained, and those that do not lead to new confirmed hypotheses should be ignored.

As an example of this activity, we might develop relations among observable individual turnover decisions and inferred internal organizational characteristics such as work group cohesiveness as indicated by assessments of member identity with work groups. From these relations we develop verbal statements about organizational commitment. These statements concerning a nomological commitment network are integrated with statements about other networks of observables and nonobservables relevant to work-group climate in an effort to integrate across networks and to uncover new relations that should be tested. Alternatively, the initial relations involving turnover might be used to suggest other, more specific observables and constructs that should also be looked at in relation to turnover. For example, work-group characteristics may influence individual turnover through their impact on motivation (which cannot be observed directly). This suggests that turnover be examined in relation to effort exerted on the job as well as to other, more specific responses, to further refine the concept of turnover. Should we fail to find a relation between turnover and effort, we will eliminate effort from the established nomological network that includes turnover.

To decide whether we have learned anything about organizations, we might assess the history of any problem area in organizational science against standards just discussed. Ultimately, what we learn from any network of relations and, hence, what we know about organizations and responses in them depend as much on fallible judgment, common sense, intuition, filtration of information, and hundreds of unproved (perhaps unprovable) assumptions as on empirical and theoretical relations. Empirically established relations and mathematical summaries of rules of correspondence do not provide knowledge. They provide the basic data we interpret. The interpretations, judgments, and assumptions of organizational scientists are knowledge. This is not the best of all possible worlds. Our biases, however, suggest that this situation should not lead to an abandonment of tough-minded, quantitative where possible, experimental organizational science and a rush to embrace experiential "knowing" as the future direction of social science. We must start with good data. If the data we interpret are seriously flawed, applying judgment processes to these data will result in less-sound knowledge than we presently have. Judgment in the absence of data results in knowledge that is even less sound.

The fact that knowledge depends on large numbers of unproved assumptions should not cause discouragement. A healthy regard for the shortcomings of our data base is sufficient. Campbell (1974) reiterates a metaphor borrowed third-hand from von Neurath by way of Quine: In this regard, we are much like sailors who must repair a rotting ship at sea. We trust all but one of the timbers while we replace that one that appears weakest. The knowledge that the timbers we trust today will be removed tomorrow because they are also rotten in no way suggests our trust was misplaced. Some assumptions must be made before any progress can occur. As organizational researchers, we make assumptions today to test particular hypotheses. Tomorrow we should test those assumptions that are testable. If we learn tomorrow that some assumptions we make today are not supported by data, we do not abandon all our previous knowledge as valueless. We do not assume that everything we know about organizations must be re-evaluated.

We should not try to generate large-scale theories that summarize all we know about behavior in organizations. Instead, we will make progress by generating limited theories and models about limited kinds of response consistencies in organizational settings. Thus, if we must retreat and re-evaluate a previously "validated" hypothesis because an assumption has proved incorrect, we need only repair the damage to small numbers of theoretical and empirical statements and summaries of consistencies. Again paraphrasing Campbell, knowledge is better than ignorance, and knowledge depends on and goes beyond common-sense interpretations of networks of relations. The better the data base we interpret, the better and more useful our knowledge will be. In this regard, the activities of theoreticians, empirical researchers, and practitioners may differ but slightly—and then only with respect to the assumed generality of their "findings" and the depth of their questioning.

Here we insist on a tough-minded Lockean approach to data collection, preserving the distinction between independent and dependent variables, insisting on the absence of common error variance in both terms, and assessing causality wherever possible. At the same time, we need not strap ourselves into the view that the data-gathering process determines data interpretation. We are Lockean in data gathering, but we can allow ourselves to be somewhat Kantian in data interpretation. It is necessary to keep in mind that the stimulus or independent variable, although objectively defined or manipulated, is subject to a different interpretation by each respondent, as well as to different interpretations by researchers trying to summarize responses. Stimuli are changed and even created by respondents (Weick, 1977). This view allows the exquisite perversity of humans to manifest itself and be taken into account in research and theory building. Occasionally a worker who has the best imaginable job will take a day off for the sheer hell of it, or a subordinate will challenge the boss's authority while admiring and respecting the boss. The error variance that plagues our lives is error variance and will remain that as long as we allow only strict S→R interpretations of data. Recognizing that individuals create and change stimuli to which they respond, as well as accepting stimuli as encountered, should enable us to deal with individuals who make "wrong" responses.

The crucial point here is that most of our explanatory concepts are products of our minds. We use them to attribute meaning after the fact. We observe a set of relations and we "explain" the observation by developing a higher-order language containing more-general concepts. The resulting summaries are generally neither rich enough to convey the entire meaning contained in their networks, nor precise enough to convey *only* relations observed. If a concept does not convey all the meaning in its network, it is deficient. If it carries surplus meaning, it is misleading. Flawed as this process might be, we argue that we have learned something when we can summarize and abstract relations contained in nomological networks. The ultimate test of whether we indeed have learned something of value is whether we can do something to an organization, a work group, or an individual and observe predictable responses as a result of what we did.

These points can be illustrated by Torgerson's (1958) discussion of the nature and importance of measurement in science. Torgerson characterizes a well-developed science as having well-defined constructs, large numbers of connections among constructs both operationalized and theoretically defined, and well-specified rules of correspondence between data and constructs. In such a science, investigators can derive logical connections between operationally defined constructs and theoretically defined constructs and then between these latter constructs and still other unobserved constructs and finally return to data to verify the appropriateness of the logic of these connections and the validity of the original operationalizations. For example, in physics a law of symmetry led to the postulation of the existence of positive and negative atomic particles before the observations that confirmed their existence. This same law led to the prediction of left- and right-handed neutrinos. In astronomy careful observations of disturbances in the orbits of Neptune and Uranus, combined with knowledge of the law of gravity, led to the prediction of Pluto long before its existence could be verified observationally. Both Pluto and Neptune were discovered as much by mathematical laws relating planetary motions to each other and by the law of gravity (an unobserved construct) as they were by telescopic observations. In these sciences, the many rules of correspondence induce a strong reality orientation in researchers and form the basis for empirical and theoretical checks on explanations of observed consistencies and deviations.

Our field is represented by a somewhat different picture. Figure 1 (after Torgerson) is a schematic representation of organizational science. The heavy vertical line is the boundary between theory and data. Constructs closest to the right side of the figure (C_1' to C_3') are those operationalized through development and specification of measurement rules. These constructs are related logically to more-abstract constructs (toward the left of the figure). Double lines from constructs to observations represent operational definitions. Solid lines between constructs represent observed relations; dashed lines represent inferred relations. Many times the operational construct is not universally agreed to be the same as the theoretically defined term with the same name. Moreover, the multiple operational definitions of C_1', C_2' or C_3' suggest that different investigators operationalizing the same theoretically defined construct differently will very likely generate conflicting and contradictory data. Many other times, constructs having different definitions and drawn from different levels of aggregation are operationalized identically (C_1' and C_2' are operationalized by the same data, D_2) or in highly overlapping ways (C_2' is operationalized by D_4, C_3' by D_5). For example, technological complexity, a construct referring to an industry or an organization, has been operationalized by aggregating individuals' reports of the complexity of their tasks—a method of operationalizing task complexity when the construct is studied from the perspective of an individual in an organization.

In addition, multiple methods of operationalizing a complex construct never give the same information. This lack of convergence and congruence among the multiple operationalizations suggests that either the construct is too complex to be represented by a single value assigned to a set of observations *or* measurement error has occurred or rules of measurement have been poorly specified. For example, different methods of operationalizing task characteristics lead different researchers to posit inconsistent di-

Figure 1. Schematic Representation of Organizational Science

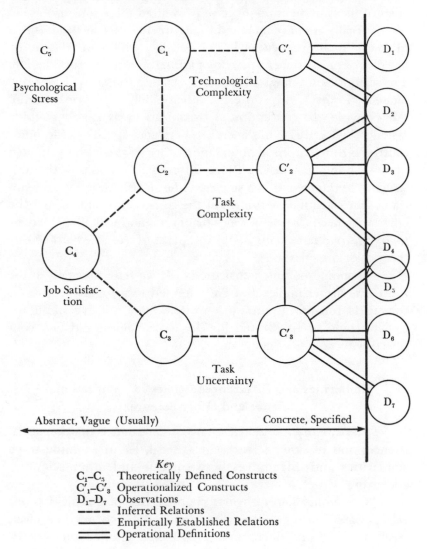

mensions of tasks. Greater precision in specifying definitions and rules of measurement might have prevented this problem.

Finally, we have included in Figure 1 a construct that is tied to no other construct either by empirically established relations or by rules of measurement-psychological stress arising from the job. The scientific usefulness of such free-floating constructs is severely limited. However, they do exist. Occasionally they prove useful. For example, the conception of organizations as loosely coupled systems (Weick, 1976) has been rarely related specifically to other constructs or to empirical observations. One of the authors, in fact, notes that on one occasion fifteen different definitions of the construct were referred to in a single two-hour discussion by academicians. The scientific usefulness of the construct is limited, but the emerging specifications of rules of observation will allow increasingly rigorous statements about the place of the construct in our theories of organizations.

It should be noted that the labels we have attached to the constructs are examples and are intended to represent classes of constructs. Job satisfaction, work-group climate, and organizational climate could be substituted for the technological and task constructs with no loss of generality.

Similarities and Differences Between Organizational Science and Other Sciences

To place organizational science in the context of other social sciences and of other sciences in general, let us examine some similarities and differences between this and other scientific endeavors.

One immediately obvious characteristic of our field is our eclecticism. Concepts, paradigms, and language are borrowed freely from several disciplines. This free and often unacknowledged borrowing has resulted in an embarrassment of riches in approaches, concepts, and meanings attached to concepts. As a consequence, we lack consensus in definitions and meanings of most of our important concepts. Another result of our eclecticism is that we use different paradigms to formulate our hypotheses (see Chapter Two). Our theoretical paradigms are not firmly established (Kuhn, 1970), a difficulty that may even disqualify our field as a "science." All this is in striking contrast to the older and better-established physical sciences.

Researchers in organizational science are more committed to studying individuals and groups *in situ* than researchers in some other social sciences. In this regard, we are more like sociologists than like most psychologists. Our greater emphasis on field studies than on laboratory studies stems from a realization that a large number of antecedents probably influence any given response consistency simultaneously. This complexity is also reflected in some models that include hypothesized intervening variables, hypothetical constructs, feedback loops, and inferred unobservable variables. Further, many relations on which our models are based are relatively weak, indicating a lack of completeness. This lack of strong and complete relations shows that we are worse off than the physical sciences and, perhaps, better off than some other social sciences.

The complexity of phenomena we investigate also leads to high tolerance for error in systems of relations. This tolerance is unhealthy. For example, as a field, we seem content with low reliabilities (perhaps in the .60s) and validities (somewhere between .25 and .30). Such contentment may be our downfall. Repeatability and reliability are the cornerstones of sciences sufficiently developed to make important contributions to society. At least one author (Fiske, 1978) argues that until social scientists are willing to devote time and energy to reconceptualizing their variables in terms of observable behaviors that can be reported to independent judges with nearly perfect agreement, we are doomed to trying to explain sets of relations so weak as to be nearly worthless. Fiske's point, though debatable, needs serious examination by researchers. Further, for practical reasons, we can never control or measure all the many antecedents of the responses we study. Thus, our systems and models are based on relatively few of the many possible *observable* relations.

For these reasons, our science is not cumulative. Today's researchers and theorists do not integrate and summarize findings from previous work to any great extent and then use these summaries as bases from which to launch their own work. Because variables change meaning and methods of operationalization from one investigator to another, integration of past work is hazardous and is undertaken only by the unnaturally brave.

Many relations we study are time- and place-bound. That is, a relation observed in an organization today may not be observed in another organization and may not be observed in the same organization next year. Although we are reasonably sensitive to environmental influences on relations, we are generally insensitive to the time boundaries of our data. The existence of time-bound relations does not mean we should give up, as has been suggested (Gergen, 1973), and content ourselves with describing the present as one point in the flow of history. It means we should conduct research that includes time in both the theory guiding the research and in its implementation. In doing so, we can perhaps learn something about establishing time intervals from historians.

Some of us at times study relations among groups that make up intact systems. For staffing purposes, we may want to learn, for example, how decisions imposed on a personnel department by the Equal Employment Opportunity Commission's testing guidelines and by public pressure affect demands placed on the training department of the same organization. In this regard, we are more like systems engineers and political scientists than like psychologists or sociologists.

Many characteristics of our field are signs of its youth. Our field is in a state of flux and is developing in a number of directions simultaneously. This fluidity and multidirectional development contribute to a lack of coherence. It should also sensitize us to the dangers of assuming beyond our capability. Our current systems for support and publication of research encourage us to imply promised benefits from our work that we cannot realistically expect to deliver. This is not just charlatanism—although there are charlatans among us—but an institutionalized kind of hucksterism that at times appears to be a vital part of obtaining research funding, establishing entree into organizations so that research can be done, and even achieving publication. Beyond this unfortunate tendency toward hucksterism, there is a kind of naïveté among us that leads us to believe that the possibilities of our science are without limit. We seem to think that if we only try hard enough, with enough time and money, our science can solve any problem. Reactions to unfulfilled promises and to threats imposed by what *might* be delivered (such as mind control through the use of drugs, or the results of behavior modification in organizations) are exaggerated by research consumers and the rest of the public. A thorough and explicit understanding of what we study and what we can deliver is essential. We usually think we know what we are about, but we are not explicit about what we are about. Unless we become explicit, we cannot engage in discussions about aspects of our field that we all agree serve to bound the science of organizations.

While some of us are interested in the pursuit of knowledge for the sake of knowledge, others are more interested in knowledge because of its uses in influencing public policy. If influence by organizational scientists on public policy is ever to come about, we must be willing to devote our energies to developing extensive empirical and theoretical bases from which recommendations can be made. Paradoxically, the hope of influencing public policy also means that where data are impossible to obtain for ethical, legal, or practical reasons, we must now make predictions without data in order that influence on public policy may occur. When we make such predictions, of course, we must be willing to state that our recommendations represent generalizations from other situations and to live with the consequences of those recommendations.

Summary

In this chapter we outlined what is and what should be done in organizational science. We noted an important reason for studying organizations and indicated the kinds of things organizational researchers and theorists should and should not attempt to explain. We emphasized observing and explaining regularities in occurrence of individual responses, aggregated responses in organizational settings, and even outcomes unique to intact groups and organizations.

Organizational science is multidisciplinary (see Chapter Two). Researchers and theorists from strikingly different backgrounds are actively pursuing knowledge about organizations Although both seemingly study organizations, researchers aggregate their data to levels ranging from individuals to entire nations. Because of this aggregation, investigators studying decisions to quit made by individual workers and those studying antecedents to volunteer terminations per 1,000 workers in a nation both label their dependent variable *turnover*. Yet we do not know whether this variable represents the same process at different levels of aggregation. A great many of our problems are caused by involving either the same or different explanatory models and theories every time we change levels of aggregation without assessing the functional similarity or dissimilarity of our models and theories across levels. Problems of aggregation will be returned to in Chapter Four. Integrating data bases, languages, models, and theories from different perspectives is well nigh impossible, given the present scattered state of our knowledge and lack of integrating framework. We will address this problem of integration further in Chapter Three.

We emphasized that attempts to understand regularities in organizations should focus on developing complex networks of relationships among multiple manifestations of multiple constructs. While acknowledging that interpretation and attribution of meanings to these complex networks are flawed and involve biases, filtration of information, and after-the-fact interpretations, we argue that this awareness should not lead us into an approach that effectively abdicates tough-mindedness in favor of introspection, experience, and phenomenology.

Finally, we discussed how the structure and approaches of organizational sciences differ significantly from other sciences. To be complete, a statement about organizational science must encompass units of analysis from individuals to interacting organizations, forcing us to borrow heavily from work done at many levels of analysis and aggregation.

By focusing on four frequently observed approaches to research and theory construction in Chapter Two, we continue our discussion of what organizational scientists do. We differentiate approaches to understanding organizational phenomena more sharply than they are probably separated in real life. At the risk of oversimplification, however, we pursue other major differentiating anatomies of organizational scientists.

CHAPTER 2

Four Worlds of Organizational Science

Organizational research entails measuring individual, group, and organizational responses even as environmental and internal processes change and place new demands on organizational components. In actuality, however, organizational researchers rarely concern themselves simultaneously with individuals, groups, organizations, and their environments, despite the broad view of organizational activity expressed by systems theorists (Berrien, 1976; Buckley, 1968; Katz and Kahn, 1966; March and Simon, 1958).

It is hard for theorists or researchers to represent organizational processes accurately, because those processes are so complex. Activities take place on several levels at once; individuals perform tasks, groups convey production norms, and organizational decision makers respond to markets. Organizational researchers and, to a lesser extent, organizational theorists try to reduce this complexity by factoring problems they address into quasi-independent parts and treating each part separately. Decomposition of complex problems into components imposes arbitrary structures on organizational activities—structures that generate convenient paradigms and simplified models of organizational activity. Each paradigm extracts and analyzes some main features of any problem but does not include all its complexity.

A small number of paradigms preeminent in the study of organizations describe the present state of organizational research and, to some extent, organizational theory. Each major discipline is generally characterized by a dominant paradigm. This chapter examines the paradigms of four major fields of organizational study: industrial-organizational psychology, human factors, social psychology, and sociology. Each discipline differs in the units of analysis studied: individuals in industrial-organizational psychology, tasks in human factors studies, individuals in groups in social psychology, and groups and organizations in sociology. Together these paradigms reflect the range of organizational activity from the individual to the organizational level.

We are not implying that these four are the only disciplines contributing to organizational science. Clearly, economists, political scientists, and historians are making contributions to this literature. Indeed, in Chapter Five we discuss at length contributions by economists to the study of turnover among organization members. An examination of all relevant paradigms generated by different disciplines is beyond the scope of this book. Salient attributes of additional paradigms will be mentioned where necessary.

The paradigms that researchers and theorists from different disciplines carry in their heads can be identified by noting the variables that each thinks control responses in organizations. In allowing researchers to focus on only a few relevant factors, these paradigms seriously limit the number and kinds of variables studied or even considered.

For example, the sociological paradigm examines the relations among such organizational attributes as task specialization, technology, and individual responses. When sociologists study the impact of specialization on conforming behavior, as postulated by

Child's (1972) theory of strategies of control, they generally do not consider individual self-esteem and desire for challenge and responsibility. However, since it is reasonable to expect that people high in self-esteem and desire for challenge and responsibility will be more willing to depart from rigid job specifications than people low in these traits, it is very likely that these traits act as moderators of the relationship between specialization and conformity. In this example, the exclusion of individual differences from the sociological paradigm leads to the omission of potentially important variables in studies of the relation between specialization and conformity.

A study designed in accordance with any of the other paradigms will likewise omit potentially important variables. Unlike the sociological paradigm, the psychological paradigm stresses the relation of such characteristics as self-esteem to individual conforming behavior while ignoring such organizational characteristics as specialization. Consequently, using the psychological approach renders it impossible to determine which, if any, organizational characteristics elicit conforming behavior in the first place. A human factors specialist might focus on the effectiveness of specialization in relation to productivity and assume that all individuals will perform the specialized tasks assigned to them and will conform to task demands. The human factors approach contains little assessment of whether individuals actually conform to the demands of specialized tasks imposed on them—an omission shared only with the sociological approach. Industrial engineers focus on objective features of the work environment and the relations of these features to productivity while assuming that individual differences are irrelevant.

Omission of one kind of variable from a given study is not necessarily a shortcoming. We do not claim that every aspect of organizational activity is relevant to every problem studied by organizational scientists. Few organizational processes, however, are so circumscribed as to rule out simultaneous interaction among individual, group, and organizational characteristics. Unfortunately, paradigm adoption has led to fairly rigid boundaries separating what is studied from what is ignored. Such boundaries hamper integration of information from different disciplines;

thus, a signal considered of paramount importance in one discipline is often ignored as noise in another. Rather than serving to limit the areas of study to those factors relevant to a particular problem, boundaries reinforce the tendency of researchers and theorists to focus on variables historically studied in their own disciplines and ignore interrelations among problems they study and those studied by others.

The boundaries resulting from paradigm adoption isolate various units of analysis: individuals, tasks groups, and organizations. Focus on some units of analysis without reference to others makes it hard for theory or research to accurately reflect ongoing organizational processes. To develop organizational theories and research designs for organizations without people or for people without organizations is unacceptable.

It may be that these paradigms are obvious and need no further explication. If this is the case, organizational scientists should see acknowledgment of these paradigmatic filters in both inferences and conclusions. We do not. Of course, every study or theory has missing variables. That some variables are systematically missing without explicit explanation is itself an interesting social phenomenon. If the paradigms are thought about, we should see in the literature concern with points of contact and integration across them. That, too, is missing.

We now outline the four paradigms. Table 1 summarizes and expands on the discussion in the following pages.

The Industrial-Organizational Psychology Paradigm

The industrial-organizational psychology paradigm is based on the premise that certain psychological processes are shared by individuals in organizations; there is sufficient heterogeneity in these processes to make them of interest. Individual differences are assumed to be more relevant to individual responses than characteristics of organizational settings are. Individual-level phenomena, such as perceptions, attitudes, and behaviors, are stressed. An example of the application of this paradigm is attitude research, in which psychologists have investigated for over fifty years relations of individual attitudes (such as satisfaction) to responses (such as performance, absenteeism, and turnover).

Characteristics of groups and organizations are largely ignored or assumed to be constant—a reasonable assumption, since usually only a single organization is examined in any one study. This fact is probably the basis of the oft-mentioned sentiment that in industrial-organizational psychology only the methods (not the findings) are generalizable. Without assessment of contexts in which people respond (and most industrial-organizational studies do not directly assess context), generalization of findings from one setting to another is difficult. Much research involves correlations of individual characteristics with perceptions, attitudes, and other responses, based on the premise that individual differences in responses to work are important in understanding individual responses in organizations.

Some characteristics of organizational contexts (such as reward systems, leadership styles, and group structures) have also been studied as determinants of individuals' responses. Studies whose designs include characteristics of work groups generally treat these characteristics in one of two ways: correlating individuals' perceptions of these characteristics with individuals' responses (as a main effect) or, less frequently, treating the characteristics as moderators of relations between individual-level variables (as an interaction, without first removing the linear effects of the characteristics).

The moderating role of contextual characteristics is an important, though late, addition in this paradigm. It probably was introduced because studies done in different organizations generally failed to yield consistent results, particularly in research on the relation of performance to satisfaction and leadership style. Situational characteristics, such as rewards for performance that are imposed by the design of the organization, have been found to moderate the relation of satisfaction to performance (Cherrington, Reitz, and Scott, 1971), and both situational and individual characteristics are postulated to moderate the relation between leadership style and employee satisfaction and performance (House and Mitchell, 1974). However, most research examining characteristics of work settings treats individual perceptions of these characteristics as predictors of individual responses rather than as moderators. Interest in the relation of individual responses to job characteristics, which are situational variables, has led to the de-

Table 1. Four Paradigms Used in the Study of Organizations

	Industrial-Organizational	Human Factors	Social Psychological	Sociological
Unit of Analysis	Individuals	Tasks	Groups and individuals in groups	Groups and organizations
Independent Variables	Personal characteristics such as sex, age, and personality; perceptions of work environment; behaviors such as absenteeism and performance; attitudes such as satisfaction and involvement	Operator skills, physical states, and mental conditions; equipment complexity; characteristics of information received by operator; attributes of work setting	Individual attitudes, perceptions, attributes, and behaviors; group morale, composition, and roles	Group variables such as sex ratio, roles, and structure; organizational variables such as size, structure, technology, and environmental factors
Dependent Variables	Attitudes such as satisfaction, behavior such as absenteeism, turnover, and performance, and self-reported psychological states such as motivation	Performance efficiency averaged across individuals	Individual attitudes, perceptions, and behaviors	Individual variables aggregated to group and organization levels such as quit or accident rates; group- and organization-level variables such as effectiveness, profitability, and structure
Focus of Measurement	Attitudes, attributes, and perceptions generally assessed at individual level; individual behaviors measured through observation and company records	Task characteristics assessed through observation; individual skills measured through task performance; performance measured by averaging across individuals performing the same task	Behavior, perceptions, and attitudes analyzed at individual level and aggregated to describe group responses and characteristics	Organizational and group variables derived from archival data, interviews with managers, and aggregation of individual variables

Boundaries Between Areas Studied and Areas Omitted	Study of individual responses and perceptions of the work setting separated from objective characteristics of the organization	Study of task characteristics and individual skills separated from individual differences in motivation and perceptions and from organizational characteristics	Study of individual and group variables separated from task and organizational characteristics	Study of organizational and group variables separated from individual responses except when individual variables are aggregated
Role of Individual	Individual-level variables are used to predict and explain individual responses	An individual's skills are considered relevant to task peformance, but psychological factors such as motivation are not	Individual characteristics are combined to describe group processes; individual behaviors and attitudes result from group processes	No individual differences in responses are considered, although individual characteristics may be combined to describe group or organizational composition
Role of Task	Individual perceptions of tasks assessed	Task characteristics studied as important determinants of performance efficiency	Not specifically studied	Studied only as related to the technology of work groups or organizations
Role of Group	Perceptions of group characteristics assessed	Studied only when interdependent tasks performed by a group of people are examined	Groups studied as important determinants of individual behaviors and attitudes and group morale and performance	Group processes studied as basis of organizational structure
Role of Organization	Organizational characteristics as perceived by individuals, such as climate, and objective characteristics, such as size or level, are studied	Only features directly related to the production process, such as technology, are studied	Organizations are not specifically studied, since no reference is made to organizational context of groups	Organizations are viewed as entities, composed of groups, that respond to internal and external processes in ways predicted by organizational characteristics

velopment of indices of job dimensions (for example, the Requisite Task Attribute Index by Turner and Lawrence, 1965, and the Job Diagnostic Survey by Hackman and Oldham, 1975). These scales measure such job characteristics as variety and autonomy. These measures of the work environment tap employees' perceptions of their own jobs and are related to individual responses to work.

Although measures of job characteristics involve employees' descriptions of their jobs and thus capture an individual-level variable, research on organizational climate, another recent addition, addresses relations of individual perceptions of *organization*-level characteristics to individual responses. Research on and theories of organizational climate exemplify the attempt to extend the industrial-organizational paradigm beyond the individual. Organizational climate is generally treated as a relatively enduring, multidimensional quality of an organization's internal environment, resulting from behaviors engaged in and policy developed by higher-level management. It is defined as an organizational characteristic as perceived by organization members (see for example, Pritchard and Karasick, 1973) and is usually measured through individuals' descriptions of organizations rather than through more-objective indicators (such as the amount of lateral or upward communication as an index of openness of communication). This subjective operationalization of the concept of climate, with little evaluation of individuals' descriptions, is thought adequate largely because it is assumed that individual perceptions of organizational characteristics are veridical. The perceptions that measure climate are sometimes aggregated to the work-group, departmental, or organizational level and are assumed to act as intervening variables in the relation of organizational characteristics to individual responses (Forehand and Gilmer, 1964; Friedlander and Margulies, 1969). Thus, it is postulated that organizational characteristics affect individual responses through their impact on individual perceptions of organizations. Operationalizing climate as perceptions is understandable as the individual is the traditional unit of analysis in this paradigm. As industrial-organizational psychologists become interested in environments in which employees work, use of individual perceptions of environments is more consistent with past practices than use of more-objective data referring to entities larger than individuals.

Because industrial-organizational psychologists operational-ize climate as perceptions by individual organization members, measuring climate is problematic. Guion (1973, p. 121) describes organizational climate as "one of the fuzziest concepts to come along in some time," since it is unclear whether climate is an attribute of the individual, the work group, the department, or the organization. Pritchard and Karasick (1973, p. 126) discuss climate as "an individual's perception of his climate," as if it were closer to the individual than to the organizational level of analysis. Measurement of climate at the individual level has also caused researchers to become concerned with the redundancy of climate with measures of individual satisfaction (Johannesson, 1973; LaFollette and Sims, 1975). This redundancy may be due to the fact that satisfaction and climate are usually assessed in the same questionnaire, capitalizing on the possibility of method bias. Regardless of these problems, organizational climate is an important addition to the industrial-organizational paradigm, because it shows a recognition of organizational environments as potential influences on individual responses.

In summary, the industrial-organizational psychology paradigm addresses individual-level variables (that is, characteristics of an individual's job and his or her responses to and perceptions of the work setting) as determinants of other individual-level responses. Industrial-organizational psychologists are trying to expand this paradigm to include organizational characteristics, but they have not yet been able to shift from the individual as the primary unit of analysis to the study of organizational-level variables. It is in the confrontation of this traditional use of individual responses with a new interest in organizational characteristics that the limitations of the industrial-organizational paradigm become evident.

The Human Factors Paradigm

Whereas industrial-organizational psychologists examine responses of individuals in organizations and emphasize differences among individuals, human factors specialists focus on relations of objective features of tasks and work environments to individual responses and emphasize differences among tasks and work settings. Objective features of work environments and operator responses have been the domain of industrial engineers and other human factors specialists since the early work of Taylor and the Gilbreths. The main concern of human factors specialists is the design of tasks to raise productivity, reduce fatigue, decrease errors, and raise performance reliability.

The major parts of the organization addressed are the equipment and the way it is used to perform tasks (McCormick, 1970). Human factors specialists try to design work to minimize waste energy and thus maximize efficiency. (Efficiency is generally defined as the ratio of work done to work done plus waste energy resulting from the process.) Much of their effort is aimed at designing production and support equipment and procedures to produce efficient work systems compatible with the physical capacities and limitations of the people who use them.

The goal is to design equipment and procedures people can use reliably. Reliability is important because of the emphasis on designing controllable and predictable work systems. The basic strategy used in work-systems design is rational, in that it stresses clear-cut cause-and-effect relations among responses of equipment operator, equipment performance, and products or results produced. Because individual differences are "designed out of" systems, differences in amount produced due to these factors are assumed minimal.

The electronics industry provides an example of production processes in which reliability is important from the viewpoint of the human factors specialist. Product quality is of major concern so that a particular organization, competing with the large number of manufacturers of similar products, can maintain its market. Because technical processes in this industry change rapidly, however, it is hard to design tasks people can perform in a consistent manner. Rapid changes in technical processes mean there are many unanticipated difficulties in implementing the processes. In response to environmental and technological demands, human factors specialists stress conformance to fairly rigid production specifications, resulting in employees specializing in a few specific tasks. The goal is to gain production reliability by increasing control over the production process.

In designing reliable systems, human factors specialists usually assume an average level of motivation, or willingness to work. The prevalence of this assumption is attributed to the predominance of military settings and problems in both field and laboratory research in this area (Swain, 1973). The redundancy of military personnel, Swain says, makes it plausible that a few highly motivated people can make up for those with little motivation. Generalizability of this assumption to industrial settings has not been shown empirically.

Although the human factors paradigm takes individual differences in skill into account, it precludes consideration of another influence on task performance: social aspects of work environments. One example is a commonly studied problem, vigilance decrement. Vigilance decrement is the decrease over time in individual performance at monitoring a set of dials or displays for infrequent changes near the threshold of detectability. In vigilance research, psychomotor activities such as responses to equipment displays, are examined in relation to task performance by combining psychophysical measures to produce indices of individual arousal levels. Despite the abundance of vigilance studies in the literature, some human factors specialists have concluded that the most important finding in this area is that vigilance decrement is not systematic and that few systems have been improved through detailed examination of vigilance (Adams, 1963; Hunt, Howell, and Roscoe, 1972). Cortlett (1973) argues that when arousal and social aspects of the work situation (such as the opportunity to talk with others while working) are considered in the interpretation of vigilance studies, the systematic study of vigilance does produce consistent and replicable results of practical significance. Since social interaction is a source of stimulation, social activities may reduce vigilance decrement: operators may stay aroused and alert longer when working with others. Thus, the current focus in human factors research on the psychophysiology of vigilance decrement without assessing social environment probably ignores a critical determinant of human performance.

In summary, the human factors paradigm assumes that a standard minimum level of ability and motivation characterizes people in organizations. Equipment, task design, and features of immediate work environments (for example, noise and lighting) are assumed to be primary determinants of task performance. The task to be performed is the main focus. Although human factors specialists, like industrial-organizational psychologists, study individual behavioral and psychophysical responses, the human factors paradigm does not consider less tangible individual differences in responses to work, such as attitudes or values, as important determinants of performance. Such variables as attitudes or values are not included in human factors research or theory. The stress is on objective features such as task requirements and equipment design.

This view leaves out characteristics of organizations not directly related to technical processes that shape tasks. For instance, it may include technological characteristics such as level of automation but will ignore centralization of decision making and other structural variables of organizations which often accompany automation. The boundary between what is studied and what is ignored falls between tasks and the organizational settings in which these tasks are found.

The Social Psychological Paradigm

Social psychology is the study of influences of social processes, such as socialization, impression formation, and group decision making, on individual responses. Too often we confuse this with the notion that social psychologists investigate group responses. Typical research in social psychology focuses on individual responses associated with differences in group characteristics.

The processes studied by social psychologists occur in many types of social systems, one of which is the complex organization. In addition, large segments of research on groups are carried out in laboratories and the results generalized to organizations. Research and theory on the development of self-perceptions of motivation (Shaw, 1977) are examples of generalization of laboratory findings to organizational settings. Students' responses to extrinsic and intrinsic rewards offered in laboratory experiments are generalized to statements about the impact of job design on employee satisfaction. Research done in small groups is often cited as empirical support for theories of organizations that address roles of groups in organizations (see, for example, Katz and Kahn, 1966).

The paradigm underlying the study of individual responses in groups is based on the premise that a group is qualitatively different from its individual members. This premise implies that a person's responses cannot be studied adequately without reference to the social groups to which that person responds. Research and theory assume that people respond differently in groups than when alone because of differences in stimuli experienced (Shaw, 1977). Of the groups social psychologists study, the most relevant to organizations are groups organized to perform some definite task or series of tasks. Although researchers and theorists differentiate task-oriented and non-task-oriented groups, they do not consider the impact of particular task characteristics such as complexity or ambiguity on responses, an omission for which they are criticized (Hackman, 1976, p. 1472).

The nature of social interactions among group members is scrutinized, emphasizing processes through which group members influence one another's attitudes, perceptions, and behaviors. Studies of group processes focus only on a few independent variables as they influence individual responses (Shaw, 1977). Physical environments (personal space or the proximity of others); group-member characteristics (age, sex, physical size, and personality traits); group composition (cohesiveness and homogeneity); and group structure (status differences and leadership styles) are the usual sets of independent variables considered in social psychological research. Owing to the emphasis on *social* determinants of individual behavior, features of tasks that groups perform and of organizations in which they exist are generally excluded from study. Thus, a boundary separates organizational and task characteristics from group attributes and individual characteristics and responses. The dependent variables studied by social psychologists are individual responses treated as products of group processes.

An example of the study of an individual-level dependent variable in relation to a group-level independent variable is Lieberman's (1956) examination of role perception as a function of organizational role. Lieberman found that individuals' perceptions of union and management were significantly related to change in role from employee to foreman or shop steward and back to employee. Note that here role is defined as a group-level variable when, in fact, others might define it as an individual variable, an organizational variable, or an interaction among two or more of these.

Individual responses to group-level variables have been used as dependent variables and may also be combined to describe groups. Cohesion, the degree to which a person is attracted to a group, is an individual response to the group. It has been used, however, as a group-level variable to differentiate among groups. For example, Seashore (1954) hypothesized that group cohesion influences uniformity in productivity. Seashore measured cohesion by averaging individual responses across group members; a measure of uniformity in productivity was derived using within-group variance of group-member productivity. Highly cohesive groups were more uniform in their productivity than groups lacking in cohesion, implying that group production standards exist and are enforced in cohesive groups. Group behaviors and attributes were derived from responses made by individuals—a characteristic feature of the social psychological paradigm. The use of aggregation, or a combination of individual responses to measure a group characteristic, indicates that responses and interactions of *individuals* are the foundation on which group characteristics and responses are based. Note that cohesion could be defined and assessed as a global variable not dependent on combining individual responses.

The social psychological paradigm can be summarized as the study of individual behavior in group and social situations in which characteristics of groups are believed to be major determinants of individual responses. Attributes of tasks performed by group members and of organizations in which groups are located are usually not studied systematically.

The Sociological Paradigm

Organizational research and theory based on the three paradigms so far discussed have at least one thing in common: they examine individual responses in the contexts of organizations (though frequently ignoring these contexts). Not all research and theory dealing with the human activity in organizations involves the study of people. The paradigm that encompasses most organizational study beyond the individual level and does not necessarily address individual responses to organizations is the sociological paradigm. Economists also usually do not focus on individual responses, but they rely heavily on aggregates of individual responses (Morgenstern, 1963).

The sociological approach to organizational theory and research is based on the premise that organizations are forms of social collectives with enduring patterns of social interaction. This definition of organizations could easily be construed as taking individuals into account, because individuals can be viewed as organisms who engage in relatively enduring patterns of responses, but the link between organizations and individuals has not been made in sociological research and theory. Social interaction is assumed to continue unaltered when individual members of the collective leave and others are added.

The social collectives that are the focus of research and theory are those social entities discussed by Parsons (1949): groups, organizations, institutions, and societies. They are ordered classes of social action in which larger collectives subsume smaller ones. The lowest level of analysis is generally the smallest social collective, the group. Because smaller social collectives are embedded in larger ones—for example, groups exist in the framework of complex organizations—sociologists examine interrelations among smaller and larger collectives. Thus, when a theorist postulates that the number of union members is related to the level of automation in an organization, a group-level variable (number of union members) is assessed in relation to an organizational variable (level of automation). The sociologist's unit of analysis is the industrial-organizational psychologist's environment.

This paradigm is picturesquely described as the examination of organizations in the manner of a sculptor (Azumi and Hage, 1972, p. 4). Here the pattern and form of human activity and human relations are explored rather than the color and detail of personality and individual differences. Since the lowest level of analysis is the group, individual differences in responses to group or organizational characteristics are not within the scope of analysis. The boundary separating areas to be studied from those to be excluded falls between the organization and the group (to be studied) and the individual (to be ignored). This exclusion of individual differences is based on the assumption that individual group members respond in similar ways because characteristics of groups are major determinants of individual responses. The best-known example of this assumption is found in Weber's bureaucratic model of organizations, in which the assumption of individuals' conformity to their roles in a formal organization is crucial to the effectiveness of the bureaucracy. Given this assumption by sociologists, if individuals conform to specified organizational roles, individual differences are unnecessary to understanding individual responses. In this regard sociologists and human factors researchers have something in common. However, divergence exists in that here characteristics of roles are important variables in studying organizational processes.

The concept "role" is the main focus of the sociological paradigm. Katz and Kahn (1966, p. 179) define role as *"one or more recurrent activities* out of a total pattern of interdependent activities which in combination produce organizational output." Sociologists attach roles to organizations—not to groups (as social psychologists do), to individuals (as industrial-organizational psychologists do), or to some interaction among organizations, groups, and individuals or between two of these. This view of roles conveys the critical concepts of interdependence and recurrent or patterned activities. The concept "interdependency" suggests that relations among roles are the building blocks of organizational activity: formal organizational roles structure performance in organizations and groups. These interdependent activities are also structural characteristics of organizations, reflecting enduring patterns of activities that are maintained despite turnover among occupants of roles. Patterns of activities studied are formal organizational processes such as division of labor, level of specialization, interdependencies between organizations, work-flow technology, and interdependence of functions; they reflect the structural view of organizations described by sociological theorists such as Perrow (1970). No distinction is made between structure and process in operationalizing organizational characteristics and activities.

The emphasis placed on organizational roles as basic structures that combine to form organizations leads to different interpretations of individual behavior than in the industrial-organizational and social psychological paradigms. In the sociological paradigm, the responses of a lathe operator to equipment problems or of a sales manager to customer demands are viewed as resulting from the roles these people occupy rather than from environmental or psychological processes. Thus, when an operator whose lathe has broken down initiates repairs, the action is interpreted as due to role specification (if the operator's job duties include equipment maintenance). Individual desire for variety or responsibility on the job would not be considered as an explanation of the action. Similarly, a sales manager's helpfulness in dealing with a customer is viewed as conformity to a role rather than as due to social rewards derived from interacting with others or expectation of monetary rewards from increased patronage.

The assumption that adopting formal roles leads to conformity is prevalent in research and theory. Any departure from conformity is treated as measurement error or ignored. However, as Child (1973) notes, there is little empirical investigation of how people respond to bureaucratic structures. In his study of the relation of organizational structural characteristics to individual responses, Child reports that decision-making centralization is related to conformity, while structuring of activities is not. Contrary to an assumption of the sociological paradigm, structuring of activities is associated with interpersonal conflict. Thus, the exclusion of individual responses in the study of social collectives appears to reflect a convenient paradigm with unvalidated assumptions rather than the absence of individual variability in conformity to social roles.

Students of social collectives investigate environments in which collectives exist and internal processes that maintain them. Internal organizational structural characteristics are often treated as summary measures describing relations among organization members (number of hierarchical levels, number of departments, ratio of administrative to production staff). Organizational structure has often been treated as a dependent variable in studies of bureaucratic models (Pugh, Hickson, Hinings, and Turner, 1968;

Udy, 1962); organizational context is assessed through measuring some combination of characteristics reflecting location, resources, and so on. More common, however, is the study of the impact of technology on structure, a major research emphasis since Woodward's work (1958, 1965). In general, most theory and research focus on relations among organizational characteristics such as structure and technology (for example, Child, 1972; Mohr, 1971; Pugh and others, 1968a and b) rather than on the relation of structure and technology to individual responses. This orientation is due largely to the historical emphasis in this paradigm on problems of organizational structuring, a result of which is comparative research on organizational attributes across a number of settings.

Although sociologists stress study of organizational characteristics, they often measure concepts through individual responses. The operationalization of the concept "technology" is an example. Technology is treated in organizational theory as an organizational characteristic (Perrow, 1970; Thompson, 1967) and is operationalized at the organizational level by a number of researchers (for example, Hickson, Pugh, and Pheysey, 1969; Woodward, 1965). However, technology has been measured at the individual level (Bell, 1967; Hage and Aiken, 1969): individual responses obtained through structured interviews or questionnaires were used to assess technology at a more macro level. Although the sociological paradigm excludes individuals from study in its theories of organizational processes, researchers often aggregate individual measures to operationalize organizational characteristics. This use of individual responses resembles the method of measuring organizational climate used by industrial-organizational psychologists and has the same limitations. Using individual-level measures to operationalize concepts of organizational characteristics introduces ambiguity into the concepts; for example, it is unclear whether technology is an organizational-level variable or an attribute of the responding individual's job or even of the individual.

To summarize, sociologists study patterns of organizational interaction without studying individuals. The difficulty the sociological paradigm evinces in excluding people suggests that the existing boundaries that separate organizational and group processes from individual processes require examination.

Four Treatments of Communication

The paradigms discussed differ greatly in units of analysis, in variables considered, and in assumptions made. To illustrate their differences more thoroughly, we describe here their approaches to studying an organizational activity for which each paradigm has been employed—communication, or the sending, receiving, and attachment of meaning to information.

In the industrial-organizational paradigm, communication research generally involves measurement of individuals' perceptions of the effectiveness of supervisors, co-workers, and subordinates at transmitting information (for example, Likert, 1967). Perceptions of communication are often correlated with individual responses such as satisfaction or stress. Industrial-organizational psychologists also study the relation of a person's position in an organization (for example, rank or supervisor-subordinate) to communication activities (for example, Roberts and O'Reilly, in press a; Sutton and Porter, 1968). Organizational features specifically related to a person's position are considered relevant to his or her communication behaviors. However, the impact of features of physical environments (for example, noise levels) or of organizations (for example, structure and technology) are not generally considered by industrial-organizational psychologists. Communication is studied as an activity performed by people and related to individual organizational position and response.

The communication problem addressed in the human factors paradigm is that of machine-to-operator communication, in which physical characteristics of machines interact with physical skills of operators in influencing communication effectiveness. The human factors specialist's main purpose in studying communication is to design equipment that human operators can use reliably. The specialist is concerned with physical characteristics of information sent. If information is complex and may take on many values, such as the temperature of a furnace, visual displays may be appropriate. However, in an emergency where operator attention is required immediately, an alarm or buzzer may be the best transmission device. The nature of information is the main determinant of the sensory channel used. Sight, hearing, and touch have been widely investigated as channels through which equipment transmits information to employees (Chapanis, 1965). If the sheer amount of information transmitted and received is of paramount importance, each bit will be transmitted once over a single channel. This means that the maximum amount of information can be transmitted per unit of time or channel. Paradoxically, it also means that the probability of any one information bit's being received without error is low. Alternatively, if accuracy is of overriding importance, each information bit will be transmitted over several channels simultaneously. This increases the probability that any one bit will be received accurately and decreases the amount of information that can be transmitted per unit of time or channel.

Human factors specialists assume that any employee using a machine has the minimum sensory levels required to receive information conveyed by the machine. In treating organizational communication, social psychologists differ from human factors specialists by focusing on the impact of social group structure on individual communication rather than the impact of physical environment. Classic laboratory studies of communication (Bavelas, 1950; Leavitt, 1951) examined the impact of group attributes (such as degree of interconnectedness among group members) on individual affect and task performance. The results were then generalized to organizations and led to field studies focusing on direction of information flow in organizations (for example, Allen and Cohen, 1969; Roberts and O'Reilly, in press b; Sutton and Porter, 1968). In these studies the importance of organizational role (for example, as superior, peer, subordinate) in shaping individual communication is considered.

As in the industrial-organizational paradigm, communication is conceived of in these studies as a product of individual responses (rather than as a product of an interaction between a machine and a person, as in the human factors paradigm). Both paradigms incorporate organizational position, but only the social psychological paradigm examines the impact of communication structures on individual responses. The reason for this difference may be that the social psychologist treats organizational position as a group attribute, the industrial-organizational psychologist as an individual attribute. The two paradigms examine the same variable (position) from different levels of analysis and then relate this variable to individual responses. The social psychologist embeds people into groups; the industrial-organizational psychologist usually does not.

Turning to examine the study of communication based on the sociological paradigm, we find striking differences. Here communication is treated as a process associated with organizational roles (as it is associated with organizational position in the industrial-organizational and social psychological paradigms). However, sociologists do not necessarily measure responses of people who occupy those roles; communication activities are *assumed* to be associated with given organizational positions. This assumption is illustrated in a study of the impact of social-system size on communication and administrative intensity (Kasarda, 1974). To operationalize the concepts "administrative intensity" and "communication," Kasarda used the proportion of residents classified as professional, technical, and clerical employees in census data. The proportion of residents classified as professionals in communities in Wisconsin was used as an index of administrative intensity, and the proportion of residents classified as clerical employees in each community was used to assess the amount of communication required to maintain social systems in the community. The use of proportion of clerical employees as an index of communication was based on the assumption that clerical employees are more likely to be found in social systems where there are large amounts of communication than in systems where there are not. Here the level of analysis is the community, and the variables size, administrative intensity, and communication are used to describe communities rather than the organizations they contain or the individuals in those organizations. Communication is assessed without reference to individuals, in contrast to the approach taken by human factors specialists or by psychologists. Kasarda's study also contains similar analyses of administrative ratios for school systems and nations, all of which assume that clerical positions represent communication. Individual differences in amount of communication activity engaged in while occupying particular organizational roles are not considered, because of the implicit assumption that differences in characteristics or responses of individuals are irrelevant to group- or organization-level activity.

It is apparent that the different levels of analysis employed in the four paradigms lead to major differences in approach to the study of communication and to different and unintegratable findings. Different levels of analysis also lead to different approaches and findings in the study of other constructs. Differences in types of communication processes studied necessitate different paradigms because not all features relevant to, say, machine-to-operator communication are relevant to social-system communication. However, the disparity between the study of an individual who passes information to another person and the investigation of information flow in a social system reflects rather clearly the particular emphases of paradigms rather than qualitative differences in the type of activities involved in transmitting information (Roberts and others, 1974).

Are not all social systems composed of people who communicate with one another? Are not all individuals who are members of social systems influenced by them? If the answer to these questions is yes, then the paradigms underlying research on individual- and system-level communication unjustifiably impose structures on such study that make it virtually impossible to generalize results from one research area to problems studied in another. The problem is one of incongruous concepts and cavalier assumptions when the processes studied may be parallel.

Conclusion

The paradigms presented describe general approaches to organizational problems taken by researchers and theorists. Explicit identification of paradigms underlying studies of organizations never occurs, but it is important, because paradigms determine appropriate units of analysis, methods of measurement, variables studied, methods of operationalization, and roles played by individuals, tasks, groups, and organizational attributes. Our refereed journals are filled with empirical work and theory development in which inappropriate methods, measurement, and analyses follow from the writer's failure to be clear about the paradigm from which he or she was operating and from failure to take broader views of concepts and problems.

Different approaches to the study of communication exemplify how paradigms affect treatment of organizational issues. Far from reflecting all factors relevant to particular organizational activities studied, paradigms act as perceptual filters that determine how students of organizations view the processes they study. Paradigms also go beyond simply limiting how we perceive organizational processes: they reinforce our limited perspectives by making it hard to integrate theories and research from one discipline with those from another.

The four paradigms discussed are the general models used in organizational research and theory today. However, political scientists and economists also study organizations. Allison's (1971) examination of the Cuban missile crisis provides a good example of the role played by decision making outside the organizational sphere in shaping public policy and events that economists and political scientists address. We limited our discussion to those fields focusing specifically on activities at the organizational level. But two questions can now be asked: "Is it possible to design research in organizations without the limitations that characterize present paradigms and without requiring researchers to study simultaneously every individual at all levels in a myriad of organizations? And is it possible to develop theories that are not so broad that they lose sight of that organizational segment with which the theorist is primarily concerned?" We answer these questions affirmatively. In Chapter Three we propose a framework that can help us choose our levels of analysis and reexamine our methods of factoring organizational activities.

CHAPTER 3

✻ ✻ ✻ ✻ ✻ ✻ ✻

Basic Concepts, a Framework, and a Dynamic Orientation

✻ ✻ ✻ ✻ ✻ ✻ ✻ ✻ ✻ ✻ ✻ ✻ ✻ ✻ ✻

Clearly there is little agreement about what constructs should be important in organizational research and theory, or we would not see the rather astonishing number of terms we do sprinkled across our scholarly journals and books. Equally disturbing is the frequent occurrence of identical terms used differently by different writers; for example, *technology* may mean "equipment," "job routineness," or both, and *structure* may refer to size but not shape or to shape but not size. Given our different paradigms, as discussed in Chapter Two, and our inabilities to move across them, this situation is not

48

surprising. It seems important to have a set of terms on whose meanings most of us can agree. These terms should be such that we can obtain linkages among them in order to halt the further drifting apart of the many rafts that hold the different contents of the social science of organizations. A modest purpose of this chapter, then, is to supply a small set of terms which we all use to one degree or another and to which we all attach relatively similar meanings.

A more ambitious purpose here is to convey the possibility that the phrase *organizational behavior,* usually used to describe our field, acts as an oar in several rafts steering us farther apart in research and theory development.

A final purpose of the chapter is to present a simple blueprint that uses the few terms discussed here and can be used later for three purposes: (1) to integrate some of the existing research in order to assess isomorphism of differently labeled constructs, differences among similarly labeled constructs, and relations among truly different constructs; (2) to help researchers design work to fill interstices between constructs; (3) to help scholars from different paradigmatic traditions begin to find and exploit their commonalities. A final purpose of this chapter is to move our thinking from a static to a dynamic view of organizations to point out some problems resulting from the current view.

Whether or not we like it (or are even aware of it), most concepts we deal with are "fuzzy" (Zadeh, 1968, 1972, 1977). Labels of sets such as "organizations" or "groups" are fuzzy, just as the concepts "much larger," "recession," and "loosely connected" are fuzzy. Our ability to deal appropriately with fuzzy concepts is limited only to the extent that our language leads us to view objects of study incorrectly. A problem we must continually wrestle with is how to tell whether a particular object, event, or constellation of characteristics belongs to a particular set. Specifying precise rules of belongingness is difficult when the criterion for belonging has been defined as possession of "very much" or "a great deal" of some characteristic (or even as presence of the characteristic, when the line between presence and absence is arbitrary). When is a driver who has been drinking drunk—how much alcohol must be in the bloodstream and for how long? When is a person unemployed—how many days or weeks must that person have been out of work? When is a group cohesive—can a cohesive group have alienated members? When is an organization effective—is an organization effective when annual profits are high but turnover is also high?

Zadeh has developed computer algorithms to handle such fuzzy concepts as "very small," "slightly," "not very large," and "very large." He suggests that no system as complex as a human being can be dealt with by traditional quantitative analytic techniques. The basis for his contention is what he labels the "principle of incompatibility." This principle says that as system complexity increases, our ability to make precise and significant statements about the system's behavior (Zadeh's term) diminishes until a threshold (presumably fuzzily defined) is reached. Beyond that tnreshold, precision and significance are nearly mutually exclusive. For this reason, precise quantitative analyses of human systems have little relevance for solving important societal problems. The full implication of this principle is not realized until a corollary principle is enunciated: that the closer one looks at a real-world problem, the fuzzier its solution.

While we agree in principle with Zadeh, our own position regarding classification diverges somewhat from his. We argue that probabilistic relations and degrees of belongingness to a set (for example, "organizations" as the set and a particular collection of people to be judged as belonging or not belonging to the set) in place of functional relations and 0 or 1 probabilities of belonging to a set can be accommodated without serious damage to inferences based on currently available statistical analytic procedures. If we can stand the ambiguities inherent in phenomena of interest to organizational researchers, analytic procedures that match the complexity of the data are available.

The situation rather resembles trying to referee a traditional ball game on a field whose boundaries, rather than being sharply demarcated, are broad zones of varying widths that fade from green on one side (in bounds) to light sprinklings of lime to solid areas of lime back to light sprinklings and finally back to solid green (out of bounds). When faced with such a situation, one has three options. One can give up the game, apply the traditional rules of the game as if everything were normal, or adjust the rules to permit continuation of the game with a minimum of confusion. To give up is not challenging. To pretend everything is normal is not rational.

A closer analysis suggests several possibilities for continuing the game. One obvious provision would be to agree that a ball hit clearly on one side or the other of the fuzzy boundary can be called with little judgment error. A ball landing on the fuzzy boundary requires a different decision-making mechanism. It might not even be too impractical to rule that the fate of balls landing on the boundary be decided by a flip of a coin or a roll of a die. Refinements can be added. The closer to the middle of the boundary the ball lands, the closer the random decision process should come to 50/50. Balls closer to the in-bounds part of the playing surface will still be judged by a random process, but the probability of being called fair increases the closer the ball is to the fair side of the boundary. Balls landing close to foul territory have correspondingly greater chances of being called foul. Explicitly introducing randomness into analytic and decision-making procedures goes against the grain of rationality in most of us. However, doing so might more nearly reflect the world of organizations and the data we derive from them than not doing so. It may therefore be useful to represent relations among constructs we study through probabilistic rather than deterministic models. It is in this spirit that we discuss a few concepts most of us use in thinking about organizations regardless of our intellectual heritages.

Individuals

Units of analyses are the entities to which responses are ascribed. As indicated in Chapter Two, the individual is the smallest unit of analysis considered by organizational researchers. Both the constructs of interest to people interested in individual responses and the paradigms they use in their research and theory development yield little disagreement about where one individual ends and another begins or about what constitutes an individual. *Individual*, then, will remain an undefined term.

Groups

Again, most of us seemingly agree about what constitutes a group. However, there is more slippage in defining groups than individuals. It is nevertheless probable that the single most important characteristic of a collection of individuals if it is to be labeled a group is that its members interact in some way. Interaction may be not only a necessary but also a sufficient condition for grouphood. Obviously, face-to-face interaction need not be the mechanism that ties people into a group, but some kind of interaction must occur.

It is often hard to tell where one group ends and another begins. One definition of a group is that its members interact with each other more frequently during some specified time than they do with other people. A search for rules setting group boundaries once and for all, just like a search for rules chiseling organizational boundaries into stone, is fruitless because our assumptions and paradigms have implicitly established those rules, as we indicated in Chapter Two. They have already circumscribed the nature of aggregations of people we study. As in any classification scheme, identification of a set of individuals as a group is always relevant to some problem or context. Among members of an organization there are groups that come about because of organizational structure and function and groups that come about for other organizational reasons. Cross-cutting these are poker-playing groups, car pools, and so on. Any one person can be, and probably is, simultaneously a member of several groups.

A concept of a group introduces a specification problem we can almost avoid facing when we limit our attention to individuals. Time plays some part in our definitions of entities. When we think about and assess individuals, there are relatively natural time intervals (such as the interval between birth and death or between one birthday and the next), which probably act implicitly to guide us in deciding *when* to assess characteristics of people and which suggest how enduring we think those characteristics are. We assume, for example, that intelligence is relatively enduring, and we can assess it once or a few times as an indicator of something a person carries through life. We also assume that affective responses are relatively enduring but are tied to situations. Affective responses may change as people change jobs, spouses, schools, or whatever. Accordingly, we often assess them when such changes occur. When we introduce the notion of a group, the role time plays becomes less obvious. Should we label as a group some conglomerate of a few people who come together for an hour once to implement a community fund-raising drive? In Chapter Four we will return to consider the role of time in specifying elements of research and theory development.

Organizations

The broadest and least confining definition of an organization is that it is a collection of people who exhibit, through some organizing process, a degree of belongingness and who are arranged in some fashion to do some thing. One process that leads to belongingness or commitment is organizational socialization. Additional constraints are usually added in order to (1) increase definitional precision and (2) address questions concerned with the organizing process. Note as we proceed that the additional constraints are usually discussed in noun terms rather than in verb terms. Thus, they further constrain our thinking to static rather than process views of organizations and are more appropriate to purpose 1 above than to purpose 2.

The additional constraints usually include the following kinds of attributes (our list is not meant to be exhaustive, as new attributes will be generated before this book is off the press). There is often a requirement that some form of communication occurs among organizational members, the notion being that without communication there can be no social organization. Other attributes against which composites of people are compared to decide whether they constitute organizations are authority or power differences, division of labor and role specification, formalization, horizontal and vertical arrangements of members, coordination and control mechanisms, centralization, goals and size.

Organizational researchers are, no doubt, in agreement that the construct "organization" itself has meanings that are somewhat more disagreed-about than do the constructs "individual" and "group." The constructs used to specify further what organizations are also carry somewhat different theoretical meanings for different writers. The problem of operationalization is less commonly discussed than is the theoretical problem of what constitutes an organization. Researchers appear to measure a construct such as centralization in whatever manner seems most opportune at the moment. A large amount of research in our field is aimed at assessing ascribed attributes and their interrelations and at demonstrating their utility in defining organizations, solving problems, and/or developing policy. We will, for the moment, accept a broad definition of *organization* and hope it will be explicated more thoroughly through future empirical work and theory development.

Since we can only specify rather broad definers of organizations, searching for organizational boundaries is clearly fruitless. One problem in trying to specify boundaries, we recall, is that in any particular research effort boundaries are at least implicitly defined in accordance with the assumptions underlying the question asked and the paradigm used in the asking. Researchers cannot identify everything that exists beyond a group of broad constructs such as those we use to amplify what we think we mean by "organization," because these constructs are not only broad, they are (loosely) tied together and act like a net; what frequently is thought to exist beyond them permeates them.

Picture a bunch of tennis balls each differently labeled. One is called "vertical differentiation," another "centralization," a third "formalization," and so on. These tennis balls are all interconnected by rubber bands; each time there is a perturbation from within or outside the system, the relation among the balls changes. (That a change in a part affects the whole is a key feature of systems analysis.) Little is known about the rules—if there are any—governing changes in relations among the balls, and little is known about the composition of the rubber bands (that is, the processes underlying connectedness among the balls). It would be hard to establish boundaries for the system of balls as a whole, because they change in response to internal and external perturbations.

We should be more explicit in our thinking that the terms and concepts generating the necessity for fuzzy logic noted by Zadeh are products of the minds of social scientists. The term *organization* is an example. The term *mental health* was generated to describe a broad set of attitudes, perceptions, and behaviors, and *leadership* was coined as a shorthand term for a large number of loosely related phenomena; the genesis of *organization* was similar. We shall probably continue to use these terms until some over-whelming evidence convinces us that the terms are dysfunctional or some set of organisms (terrestrial or extraterrestrial), studying the same populations we do, shows that they can function adequately as scientists without these concepts. That time plays an important but rarely explicated role in our own generation of concepts, measures, and theories should be even more obvious when we look at the way we defined *organization*. For example, for an entity to be classified as an organization, it usually must be shown that in the entity com-munication occurs and roles are specified. Communication over what time period? Can role specification be emergent, or must it be complete? What kinds of time intervals are involved in specifying roles?

How are organizations distinguished from groups? The most obvious distinguishing characteristic is that many organizations can be disaggregated into groups, whereas it should not be possible to disaggregate groups into organizations. Similarly, one can aggregate groups into organizations, but it should not be possible to aggregate organizations into groups. The direction in which aggregation can occur is the only singularly different attribute of groups and organizations. Each other attribute mentioned in our discussion of organizations can also be used to describe some groups. One theoretically and empirically unresolved question is how many of these attributes an entity must have before it is called an organization, not a group. For example, if we describe a collec-tion of people as highly centralized and hierarchally differentiated with a high degree of role specialization, the aggregate is more likely to be called an organization than a group. (It could also be called a family.)

It is common in our field to investigate divisions of General Motors, squadrons of the United States Air Force, units of the National Guard, and branches of Chase Manhattan Bank as though they were independent organizations. In terms of hierarchy, of course, they are not. In such organizations freedom to manipulate attributes is not present to the degree that it might be in more autonomous organizations. Are these organizations only groups? No, because there are implied, untested assumptions that the presence or absence of attributes (number unspecified) in some fundamental set differentiates groups and organizations. The assumptions remain implicit in our research, but failing to specify assumptions about what attributes and how many must be present for a group to be an organization can yield misleading research implications.

For example, Blau and Schoenherr (1971) investigated a number of structural elements in fifty-three employment security agencies in the United States, Puerto Rico, and the Virgin Islands. "These fifty-three state agencies . . . operate under federal laws and some federal supervision" (p. 11). Differentiation, administrative ratios, and decentralization were among variables of interest to these authors. One assumption in the research is that social structures show regularities that can be studied apart from a knowledge about the people in them. This may be true—and, for the moment, we will disregard the fact that incomplete pictures of organizations are obtained when their members are ignored. A key point here is that the bureaus studied are mandated by federal law, a status that often imposes structural constraints. Blau and Schoenherr address the question of the degree to which their results might be generalizable to other organizations by investigating yet another kind of government agency. If the authors had more clearly specified how the subunits are constrained by their parent organizations, it would have been easier for the reader to draw inferences about the degree to which the structural characteristics in this research might have been imposed differently than the same structural characteristics studied in more autonomous organizations or in organizations in which hierarchical constraints are different.

Environments

The simplest possible definition of an environment is that it consists of everything outside the boundary of the primary unit of focus to the investigator, if the boundary of that unit can be found. Thus, the environment for an individual is everything outside him or her. An organization's environment is everything outside it. As is obvious to us all, while gaining in simplicity, such a definition provides little guidance for constructing theory or research that takes environments into account.

A more useful definition of environments for our purposes includes a specification that they provide ambient stimuli that impinge on, and can be detected in, units of interest. For one system to act as the environment for another system, there must be a means of natural influence from the first system to the second (Klausner, 1971). This criterion both restricts potential candidates for inclusion in assessments of environments and requires that researchers and theorists begin the process of hypothesizing variables and constructs that allow for or mediate the influence of one system or another. The criterion also suggests that choosing environmental attributes that are conceptually far removed from the units of focus creates serious problems for researchers and theorists. When distant environmental attributes—the gross national product, for example—are selected, specifying mechanisms by which they act on the units of focus may be so difficult that researchers either abandon their efforts or simply correlate environmental attributes with activities of units of focus in a purely descriptive manner. This strategy can only produce a relatively sterile collection of actuarial studies having little to do with understanding processes underlying relations.

Another problem in defining and assessing environmental characteristics is alluded to in our discussion of organizational boundaries. This problem is most clearly stated in another context by Piaget (1971, p. 37): "Behavior is at the mercy of every possible disequilibrating factor, since it is always dependent on an environment *which has no fixed limits and is constantly fluctuating*" (emphasis added). Our view is more optimistic than this. We argue that even though environments constantly fluctuate, they do so lawfully and predictably. Since whole environments cannot be quantified, why not quantify aspects of environments? Characteristics of environments can be measured.

We must bear in mind that as the units of interest selected change from individuals to organizations, our ideas about appropriate environmental characteristics must concomitantly change. Variables that are specific and focused enough to have impacts on individuals may be too insignificant to be relevant to larger aggregations of individuals. Appropriate environmental characteristics defining ambient stimuli for organizations may be so general that they fade into the "background noise" not noticed by people. This point is related to our discussion of the necessity of thinking about means of natural influence. For example, an appropriate environmental characteristic for the proprietor and three clerks in a small independent grocery store may be the number of people in the surrounding area out of work owing to a layoff at the local General Motors plant. For the General Motors plant, however, the relevant environment may be reflected more appropriately by regional or national economic indicators of recession, characteristics that have an impact on the small store, only by way of their mediated influence through the local General Motors plant.

Research concerned with environmental impacts on organizations or on people in them has been popular only for the last decade. Such investigations suggest another characteristic of research in our field. Researchers are generally so intent on looking at a particular unit (individuals, groups, or organizations) that they ignore external influences on this unit. But for a number of years organizational theorists have actively stated a concern for the characteristics of the place in which an organization or an individual operates. In their treatment of environments, theoretical statements are more complete than empirical investigations. We are now seeing in our research designs concern for specification of environmental characteristics that may impinge on units of primary interest.

One way to assess a particular researcher or theoretician's assumptions about the importance of studying the environment is to ask the person to describe what constitutes the environment. The description will be fuzzier than that of the unit of primary interest (unless the researcher is specifically interested in the relation of environments to group processes, as some sociotechnical researchers are). Implicitly this suggests that writers in this field see environments as having only secondary influences on units, compared with the characteristics of the units themselves. If researchers thought environments had equal or greater influences on units, would not those influences more frequently be included in research designs and investigated simultaneously with unit characteristics?

Responses

Many macro-oriented organizational scientists take organizational positions or roles as the basic building blocks of organizations. When they discuss organizational processes, however, they borrow from their more micro-oriented colleagues the term *behavior*. Organizations, then, "behave in ways to maximize their viability." Organizations "make decisions," they "learn," and they "develop." Organizations are imbued with a life of their own. And a hidden assumption underlying this way of thinking, one frequently illustrated by the way research is done, is not merely that organizational presence is continued regardless of changes in membership but that organizational presence would be continued in the absence of members. Doubtless few organizational scientists believe this. Hence, the use of anthropomorphic descriptions of organizations is hazardous to the development of our understanding of organizational make-up and processes.

While our language determines our thought processes, it also reflects them. Anthropomorphizing legitimized by thinking about organizations as behaving, rational entities detracts from a more realistic view: that although organizations seem to be something different from a simple aggregation of their parts, they are not living entities but are entities of some other type in which processes occur.

One of our jobs as organizational scientists is to identify these processes, and this cannot be done if we describe organizations using the same language we use to describe people. Such descriptions lead to assumptions that processes operating in organizations are identical to known processes governing individual viability and that we really understand organizational processes to the degree that we understand human physiology. For example, in attempting to understand throughput problems, we make observations of the relations among organizational departments. We fail to develop a complete picture of the process of interest because we imbue organizations with the capability to act, failing to specify the activities of individuals who shape throughput. We forget that what ultimately results in something that looks like a process is the combined activities of individuals. The process would be more completely understood if the macro view (for example, examining interdepartmental relations) were combined with analyses of the activities engaged in by people that ultimately reach an observable threshold and are then labeled a process (for example, throughput).

We tend to treat entities known to be dynamic as relatively static. Anthropomorphizing, we frequently think of such phenomena as organizational learning as slow. This habit masks from view the many activities occurring, perhaps over long periods, that ultimately manifest themselves in something that looks like learning. One alternative might be to take the "Mexican jumping bean" approach to organizations. Think of an organization as a set of small, opaque boxes with covers. The boxes are connected more or less closely to one another. Each box is occupied by one or more Mexican jumping beans, but we do not know that. We see the boxes jump, but because we are unsophisticated in our understanding of organizational processes, we do not know why they jump. We observe, however, that one result of the jumping is to move some boxes closer together, some farther apart—an activity clearly different from the jumping of an individual bean. We also observe a box in which bean jumping is associated with the lid's flying off. We do not know what combination of jumping activities caused the lid to fly off or what caused the jumping. We do know enough not to attribute the flying about of box lids to a decision made by a box to "blow its top."

The term *organizational behavior* also contributes to the making of misleading statements by those of us who view organizations from a more micro perspective. We frequently label as behaviors everything we can attribute to individuals. Thus, intentional responses, unintentional responses, and affective states are all thought of as behaviors, or at least as behavioral predispositions. Although an individual's responses to a questionnaire concerned with attitudes may be behaviors, attitudinal states and processes are not. We must differentiate among internal processes, intentional responses, and unintentional responses if we are ever to tie individuals into organizations.

That our argument is valid is illustrated by the definition of *behavior* as "manner of conducting *oneself* in the *external* relations of life; demeanor, deportment, bearing, manners." *Behave* is defined as "to bear, comport, or conduct *oneself;* to act. . . . Formerly a dignified expression, applied for example to the bearing, deportment, and *public* conduct of *persons* of distinction" (*Compact Edition of the Oxford English Dictionary,* 1971; emphasis added). As organizational scientists we are interested in processes and activities beyond the public conduct of persons. And we might ask ourselves whether organizations have demeanor, deportment, bearing, and manners.

Another question we might ask ourselves, as subgroups of us frequently do, is "Does it matter what we call ourselves?" If we understand that labeling ourselves organizational behaviorists (though the authors prefer the word *scientists, theorists,* or *researchers*) only separates from other social scientists those of us interested in organizations, then it matters not how we are labeled. But if the way we label ourselves constrains and directs the way we look at organizations, the label is misleading. Organizations do not behave. People do behave. People also exhibit responses that are not intentional or even public, they carry with them emotional states, and they engage in emotional processes.

The situation may be analogous to that brought to our attention by the black movement and, more recently, the women's movement. If we label a person of African descent "colored" or "nigger" or "negro," do we think of that person in different ways than if we label the person "black"? Over generations, have the words *colored* and *negro* picked up excessive meaning that contributes to one's impressions of what such a person is? Similarly, does talking about "mankind" and "the nature of man" unconsciously eliminate from consideration over half the world's population?

We prefer to substitute the word *response* for the word *behavior* because we think if reflects more accurately what both micro-oriented and macro-oriented organizational scientists observe. What can be observed includes both intentional and unintentional activities. To talk about responses covers for micro-oriented scholars both external actions and internal processes. For the macro-oriented, the term *response* may direct attention more precisely to underlying processes governing those responses— processes that are always some combination of what people are, what they do, and the roles they play. The definition of behavior focuses almost exclusively on its public nature whenever the definition of response does not.

In English a response is defined as "an *answer,* a *reply.* An *action* or *feeling* which *answers* to some *stimulus* or *influence.*" To respond is "to *answer* or *correspond* to (*something*); to *reciprocate.* To *answer* by some *responsive act;* to *act* in *response* to some *influence.* To give satisfaction [United States–developed usage]." *Respond* is from the English *respound,* "to reply" (*Compact Edition of the Oxford English Dictionary,* 1971; emphasis added). The term *response* reflects our interest in dynamic aspects of organizational life and in causal relations. It suggests both a focus on underlying predispositions and an interaction wherein a response can serve as a stimulus to yet another response.

Tasks

At the simplest level of definition, tasks are discrete actions required of individuals by organizations of which they are members. Tasks provide an interface between an individual and a supraordinate organization. This interface is a mechanism through which organizations and their members influence each other. As noted in Chapter Two, tasks are studied as major components of organizations by industrial engineers and are becoming increasingly important, although in strikingly different ways, to industrial-organizational psychologists.

For an accurate description of an organization and its internal processes, identifying both required tasks and organizational members who carry out those tasks is critical. Task descriptions should include the sets of characteristics associated with the tasks: task content (required behaviors—for example, adjusting a dial); objective task characteristics (dimensions along which many tasks can be expected to vary—such as complexity or difficulty); and psychological dimensions, or perceived task characteristics (for example, variety or autonomy). Task-content dimensions as described by industrial engineers and perceptions of the same tasks by people performing them should covary, but isomorphism between one kind of description and the other is not expected. Since tasks form the basis of an organization's internal activity, one cannot study organizational processes accurately without reference to task attributes, their interrelation, and task performance. Similarly, required tasks are probably one of the most salient internal organizational characteristics for determining individual responses.

Problems in explicating the role of tasks in organizational functioning are related to confusion surrounding (1) relations of tasks to jobs and (2) levels of analysis of tasks. To differentiate a job from a task, a job is defined as the total set of required responses performed by a person in an organization. Many persons may hold the same job because they perform the same tasks. Any given job can, and probably does, require performance of numerous tasks in which required responses differ markedly. Jobs differ from tasks in that the required responses that make up a job need not be similar or produce the same product. The job requiring typing, filing, answering the phone, and making coffee consists of four dissimilar tasks. The concept "task" also describes related activities performed by group members that produce a joint product (drafting a grant proposal by a team of scientists, for example). All individuals on a work team need not hold the same job to be working on a common task.

When tasks are studied at the group level, the issue of levels of analysis is introduced. At least three levels of analysis are possible: intraindividual (the study of one person's performance of different tasks), individual (the study of one person's performance of a single task), and group (the study of the performance of a number of persons who work jointly on a common task). The study of larger entities such as departments or organizations contributes additional levels. The complexity introduced by considering relations among tasks simultaneously across these levels may prove overwhelming.

We have defined a minimum number of concepts in an effort to generate a parsimonious language most of us can agree on regarding meaning, syntax, and interrelations. (The need to generate a parsimonious set of terms for use in further discussion is based on the profusion and confusion of terms we see in the academic organizational literature.) Implicitly, then, we regard as important elements in organizational science *individuals,* performing assigned *tasks* and making organizationally relevant *responses,* within the context of *groups* (or sometimes performing group tasks as interacting rather than coacting individuals), located in *organizations,* which are in turn located in economic, physical, and social *environments.* The analysis of how selected characteristics of the constructs named by these terms interact and influence each other is the primary concern of organizational researchers.

A Framework

The paradigms discussed in Chapter Two and the terms introduced earlier lead us increasingly to view organizations as static. This unfortunate view is surely reflected in our research and, to a lesser degree, in our theorizing. No doubt, we would be better off if our paradigms and terminology encouraged a more dynamic view of organizations. That the paradigms in Chapter Two lead to the terminology selected here is obvious. We cannot reinvent our field by introducing a new language and, thereby, startlingly new paradigms. In fact, our intent is almost the opposite. It is to select, from an overwhelming number of elements intrinsic to paradigms guiding research and theory development, a smaller set of terms agreed on in meaning and useful in tying together work based on different perspectives. If we agree that the terms discussed are a parsimonious set of those used by most organizational scientists and that they are resonably defined here, then it might be possible to use them to develop a very simple blueprint, or framework, that can guide our evaluation and integration of past research and theory and can be used to design research. Such a framework is a set of simple specifications that indicate how one might categorize attributes and responses of interest. Although it lacks the characteristics of a model or theory, it may encourage more-inclusive research than we currently see. We will return to the problem of static versus dynamic approaches to organizations later in this chapter and again in Chapter Four.

The framework we use merely makes explicit that responses should be thought about as a function of units making them and of the environments of those units. It is stated by the equation

$$R = f (U, E, U \times E)$$

where R represents an array of responses, U a set of characteristics of the responding unit, and E a set of characteristics of the environment. This framework is a descendant of Lewin's (1951) statement that behavior (B) is a function of a person (P) and his or her environment (E). There are several important differences.

R is substituted for B and represents responses. The substitution indicates that organizational scientists are interested in responses other than behaviors, as discussed earlier. Responses, unlike behaviors, may characterize an individual or a unit larger than the individual, such as an organization. For example, organizational growth is a reflection of a variety of activities engaged in by people in the organization growing. Whatever the response of interest, we assume it reflects a broader underlying response tendency, and one of the tasks of researchers and theoreticians is to identify such broader tendencies. For example, we invoke the term *attitude* to think about response tendencies underlying an individual's response of hiring or not hiring a minority-group member. We have less conceptual help in identifying response tendencies underlying organizational growth or decline. Our stress that R should be an array of responses reflects the fact that responses are made—and should be studied—in relation to other responses, not as single, discrete acts. That they are often considered discrete acts is clear from the empirical organizational literature.

U is substituted for P to make explicit that responding units can be other than individuals. Thus, groups and organizations are appropriate units of focus. U is a vector describing relatively enduring characteristics of the responding unit.

E is a set of assessments of environmental characteristics. The set of environmental characteristics refers to objective representations of environmental variables *assessed independently of the responding units under investigation.* Insistence on independent assessment is a significant departure from Lewin's original formulation. It is a result of our growing uneasiness with relations that seemingly depend on the presence of similar sources of error in predictor and response variable sets. Journals and books are filled with reports of studies whose results are questionable because of the high probability of error attributable to using the same methods to assess all variables. Measurement purity is obtained at significant cost, since, as we noted earlier, processes through which different observations are related to one another must now be postulated and assessed wherever possible. The gain seems worth the cost. Characteristics of the environment as perceived by organization members should be differentiated from objective characteristics of that environment. Only when we make this differentiation will it be possible to determine whether variance in responses is more attributable to objective or perceived environmental characteristics.

U is multiplied by E in accordance with the hypothesis that unit and environmental characteristics, besides influencing responses separately, may interact with each other to influence responses. In the few studies that have looked for such interactions in organizations, the influence of interactions on responses has been small relative to the direct influence of unit and environmental characteristics. This lack of statistically significant interactions in the empirical literature does not detract from their potential importance. We probably have failed to find unit/environment interactions because we collect our data at one point in time and such interactions reflect continuous processes. We also probably fail to find them because we usually fail to look for them.

An important technical point must be made about the term U × E. The number of interactions that *could* be investigated is equal to the product of the number of environmental characteristics and the number of unit characteristics. Therefore, except in studies that investigate very few antecedents or predictors, the number of interactions will often be so large as to preclude rigorous study. In such situations we are reduced either to "fishing expeditions" or to heavy reliance on theory in our explorations. The potentially overwhelming number of interactions can best be reduced through careful application of limited theories and models. Empirically reducing the number of terms in E and U sets without simultaneously considering Rs is dangerous because taxonomies arrived at in this manner lack theoretical and conceptual underpinnings as well as relations with Rs of interest.

One might ask whether we need a framework at all. In one sense at least, this framework is a truism. The alternative assertion, that responses are not a function of characteristics of responding units, environments, and possibly interactions between the two, cannot be true. All we need to disprove the alternative assertion is one study that establishes relations between a set of responses and characteristics of the responding units and their environments. Such studies exist. That the framework is a truism does not diminish its value if it leads to research designs that explicitly consider the complexity and nature of multiple influences on reponses and the interrelations among responses. Any framework is useful if it can help us examine existing research to note gaps in knowledge. The major point of this framework is to encourage consideration of responding units and environments and their interactions *simultaneously* rather than continuing to stress and to study only one source of influence on responses, thereby necessarily neglecting the possibility of interaction. By examining published literature in our field, the reader can answer the question whether we need some device to encourage a broader perspective.

The argument for increased breadth in research designs is strengthened when one considers as an example the theoretical controversy about situation/person interaction in personality and social psychology. Studies done in organizational settings can contribute to the resolution of this debate. The question being asked in this research—"Which attributes influence responses: those of situations or those of individuals?"—is the wrong one. By carefully choosing (or manipulating) situational, individual, and response variables of interest, we can generate data to support either side of the controversy, both sides, or neither side. However, by maintaining distinctions among variable sets and including in research variables from all sets, we can answer the more carefully posed theoretical question "Which responses are uniquely controlled by unit attributes, which are controlled by environmental attributes, which are controlled by a combination of both, and which are not related to either?" The specific relations of responses to unit, environmental, or both kinds of attributes should give us some insight into the unobservable processes the underlie these responses.

Increasing the breadth of organizational research has practical significance as well. It is important to know which responses are controlled by what is brought to the situation and which responses are controlled by what is found there. If, for example, worker productivity is controlled by the attitudes and characteristics that workers bring to the work situation, attention should be concentrated on selection programs, preemployment training programs, or other vestibule activities. If productivity is controlled by what is in the situation, more attention should be given to activities like organizational design than to activities like selection.

Finally, demonstrations of transsituational stability of relations between unit characteristics and responses are essential if we are to make any progress toward resolving the question of the relative usefulness of general and of situationally specific theories. Such demonstrations cannot be provided in the absence of specification of environments.

Assumptions Underlying Our Thinking

Just as we have tried to identify the assumptions underlying the terminology of our field and the nature of currently available research, we should uncover assumptions that govern organizational scientists' thinking.

First, we assume that even though we often cannot demonstrate causality, every response is caused by something. Further, responses are caused by something in the responding unit or in its environment.

Second, we assume that organizations and their subunits are unique. Of course, so are identical twins, containers of gas, and mass-produced political campaign buttons. Just as these other entities can be described using a large number of terms so too can organizations. However, we assume these other entities and organizations can also be described by a much smaller underlying set of dimensions. A closely related assumption is that a relatively small number of homogeneous sets of responses exist that summarize most of the nearly infinite number of observable responses. More empirical and theoretical attention must be given to identifying these sets of related responses so that we do not go about the hopeless task of trying to understand everything. As it is, we are in a situation in which we measure many things people do in organizations as well as organizational attributes with little understanding of which responses and attributes are trivial and which are important.

Simultaneously with identifying important homogeneous response sets, we must link these responses to nonresponses in an attempt to identify processes intervening between nonresponse and response factors. The alternative is to continue to analyze only a few correlates of a large number of responses without knowing the importance of the correlates or the functional similarity of the responses. This practice constitutes poor science and inefficient research. Our assumption is that there are a small enough number of dimensions that we can understand their relationships; the processes governing them are open to question. This assumption should be subjected to theoretical and empirical scrutiny.

A further assumption is that even though organizations are unique, nomothetic studies of them are likely to be valuable. Organizations do have some qualities and dimensions in common with one another. The truth value of this assumption is irrelevant when one considers research activity that would result from the opposite assumption. If we assume that because organizations are unique, generalizing what is found in one organization or sample to another organization or sample is not valid, then all organizational research should be of the single-organization or case-study variety, with no attempts at generalization. If generalization from nomothetic studies proves invalid, the damage caused by conducting such research is inexpensively repaired. Information about single organizations can always be drawn from compiled data gathered in a nomothetic study, through disaggregation. The opposite is usually not possible. Aggregating case studies, if generalization proves possible, can be accomplished only in the unlikely event that all the case studies are conducted identically and all relevant data obtained using identical measures are available for each organization. Case studies should be used to generate hypotheses, not to test them.

Yet another assumption is that individuals are the basic building blocks of organizations. Their responses can be assessed and aggregated. But these aggregated responses are not assumed to be responses made by groups or organizations. Further, we assume that there are responses uniquely attached to groups and organizations. Cohesiveness, for example, is not something an individual displays. It is uniquely attached to groups and is assessed differently than is individual friendliness, which may contribute to it. Whether friendliness and cohesiveness are the individual and the group manifestations of the same underlying process is an empirical question.

Our final assumption is that unit responses and characteristics must be at the same conceptual level and that environmental characteristics associated with them be conceptually close to the unit responses and characteristics. For example, we would not study interrelations among national unemployment rate, gross national product per capita, and working days lost through strikes in an attempt to understand the processes underlying individual job dissatisfaction. We might investigate these national characteristics in preparation for specifying organizational policies concerning quality of working life. The complexity of one's research approaches and strategies should match the complexity of the questions asked.

From Static to Dynamic

The framework presented here has a static meaning because of its brevity and because of our field's historical lack of attention to change. Most research in our field is static. Most studies are fleeting glances (analogous to stop-action photographs) at organizations. In those rare studies in which observations are made more than once, the pictures are taken at arbitrary time intervals. These practices generate infrequent and poorly focused attention to change. When we make an observation at only one point in time, we lack the opportunity (or perhaps the motivation) to describe how changes at time 1 influence responses at time 2 or why responses along the same dimensions are different at times 1 and 2. The notion of time has yet to be entered into our equations.

The pervasiveness of this problem may be emphasized by noting a passage from Pat Jordan's autobiography: "My career was no esthetically well-made movie—rising action, climax, denouement. It was a box strewn with unnumbered slides. A box of pure and frozen moments through which I have been sorting, picking up a moment here, a moment there, holding them to the light, seeing previously undefined details, numbering that moment, then putting it with all the others in some order which, I hope, will eventually produce a scenario of my career. . . . Sitting here, I can see Jim Hicks, fallen to one knee [from the force of his swing]. He glares at me through time and space" (Jordan, 1975, p. 169).

Such stop-action photographs serve organizational scientists no better than they do autobiographers. They fail to indicate the ordered sequence of events; the problems of stopping a process to measure it are glossed over; the problems of putting the slides back together to form a sequence are unresolved. At freezing the unsorted memories of the moments of his career, Jordan was a master. Yet vivid memories or frozen moments do not capture a career or a process, nor do statistical interactions make a sequence. We, no different in may respects from novelists or biographers, observe randomly chosen moments of time, frozen because of the arbitrary, one-shot nature of our research. Within these random moments we observe varying degrees of fineness of detail dictated by the resolution capabilities of our lenses. From these flawed and arbitrary data we attempt to re-create processes that generate response tendencies.

The inferred tissue that connects the jumble of slides constituting Pat Jordan's memories and thus enables him to reconstitute his life is fundamentally no different from the set of inferences we make to lead us from physically measured or manipulated stimuli to evoked responses. The biographer, in order to describe the passage of his protagonist through life, makes the same inferences about continuity of time, space, individual characteristics, and even matter qua matter that we make.

In other context, Fiske (1978, p. 167) notes that time plays an essential role in modern physics, especially in relativity theory.

> In biology, large orders of time are involved in evolutionary studies, and extended periods must be included in developmental investigations. Physiology examines rather rapid processes, and neurology studies even more rapid ones. Economics involves temporal ordering, especially in econometrics. Time plays a central role in areas of psychology that seem to have made progress, such as conditioning, learning, and perception.
>
> Some natural sciences, as they have progressed, have brought smaller and smaller units into their investigations. For example, biology has proceeded from studying organisms to studying organs, from organs to cells, and from

cells to their components and to molecular processes. Shorter and shorter time periods also appear to be involved. Physics is now concerned with particles that exist for only infinitesimal parts of a second; biology has moved from examining physiological processes of comparatively long duration to chemical processes that are almost instantaneous. Although the scientist can construe processes with either long or short invervals between their stages, improvements in observing and measuring have enabled him to study processes with shorter and shorter durations.

When researchers do look at relations over time, they are usually arbitrary in specifying time intervàıs of interest. For example, one might be interested in observing organizational growth or decline annually for five years. It might even be possible to demonstrate for some set of organizations systematic patterns of growth or decline. The missing link is specification of why the particular time intervals chosen are important or even relevant (an issue that will be returned to in Chapter Four). This link can be made only by specifying the theoretical basis for the choice of the intervals.

The introduction of time changes our framework from static to dynamic. It is possible that adopting the expanded version of the framework will require researchers to specify mechanisms they think operate through time. Once these processes are specified, hypotheses can be developed that test their comparative utilities.

Our original framework is

$$R = f (U, E, U \times E)$$

A response at time 1 is a function of the characteristics of the responding unit, the characteristics of the environment in which the unit operates, and possibly the interaction of unit and environmental characteristics:

$$R_1 = f (U_1, E_1, U_1 \times E_1)$$

Now, the response can alter the characteristics of the unit at time 2, a course of events we express as $R_1 \rightarrow \Delta U_1 = U_2$. Or the response can alter the characteristics of the unit's environment: $R_1 \rightarrow \Delta E_1 = E_2$. Or the response can alter characteristics of the unit *and* of the environment. Changes in the unit, the environment, or both will mean that the unit will respond differently at time 2 than at time 1, so that

$$R_2 = f(U_2, E_1, U_2 \times E_1)$$

or

$$R_2 = f(U_1, E_2, U_1 \times E_2)$$

or

$$R_2 = f(U_2, E_2, U_2 \times E_2)$$

If no change occurs in U or E between time 1 and time 2, then

$$R_2 = f(U_1, E_1, U_1 \times E_1)$$

The new response (R_2) can contribute to still further changes. Thus $R_2 \rightarrow \Delta U_2 = U_3$. Similarly, $R_3 \rightarrow \Delta E_3 = E_4$, and so on.

In attributing changes in U and E to responses, we are detailing a closed-system paradigm. In actuality, U and E changes are often attributable to influences other than responses. Nevertheless, that U's and E's should be assessed at every stage at which responses are observed seems obvious in light of the probability that they do change and therefore influence responses differently at different times—influences we frequently gloss over by observing unit and environmental characteristics only once (and maybe then not in the same time period in which responses are assessed) and assuming their stability. The stability of most U and E characteristics should be an empirical question for organizational researchers. As indicated, any combination of stability and change in Us and Es is possible.

Such notations as $R_1 \rightarrow \Delta U_1 = U_2$ and $R_1 \rightarrow \Delta E_1 = E_2$ direct our attention to the need to specify the processes through which responses change units and environments. After those processes are specified, researchers can make intelligent guesses about time intervals necessary for an expected change to occur. Selection of time intervals between measurements need not be as arbitrary as it now is.

The additional notation also encourages us to think about whether responses influence units or environments at all and whether the unit or the environment is influenced more. If responses are expected to influence some aspect of units (as they certainly are in behavior modification research) but instead prove to influence only environments in which units operate, one should develop theories and programs that focus on environmental, rather than unit, change. Alternatively, if a set of responses changes units but not environments, ensuing observations of those responses can be made more efficiently by eliminating from concern environmental characteristics, and programs to bring about change should focus on units. Neither unit nor environmental characteristics can be ignored in subsequent observations if the impact of responses on them is not considered in initial observations. Thinking about the expanded framework leads us to devote more attention to processes while still keeping units of observation distinct. Focusing singularly on units and their environments leads to the structural view of organizations inherent in our paradigms. Attending to responses, time, and things that aggregate through time to produce responses forces us to include processes in research and theory development, simply because we have to think about how R's might translate into changes in E's and U's and, concomitantly, how U's and E's change R's.

As an example, consider a research question concerned with interorganizational relations. Some researchers look at such relations from an exchange perspective that states that the motivation to interact is symmetrical: organizations come in contact when leaders in both organizations perceive it to be in their best interests to be in contact. Interorganizational interactions are characterized by cooperation. Other researchers follow a power-dependency approach that implies asymmetrical motivation to interact. That is, leaders in one organization are motivated to interact, those in the other are not. Interaction occurs when there is sufficient power in one organization and not in the other that inducements to interact made by members of the first organization are successful. Interactions are characterized by conflict and bargaining.

Some researchers are interested in developing an integrated view of interorganizational interactions, incorporating the basic propositions from both the exchange and power-dependency models (Schmidt and Kochan, 1977). These researchers have developed hypotheses about frequency in interaction and the degree to which interaction is characterized by conflict or cooperation in symmetrical and asymmetrical situations based on perceived benefits of the interactions by members of interacting organizations.

One could place the general question of this research into the framework provided here and assess the degree to which the framework helps us focus simultaneously on a number of complementary questions about interactions among organizations. For our example we select sets of organizations in which there are varying degrees of interaction across members. The dependent variables (or responses) are amount of interaction members of focal organizations have with members of some other organizations and degree to which that interaction is characterized by cooperation, conflict, or bargaining. Unit characteristics include perceptions by members of focal organizations about the degree to which interaction with any other organization or its members is beneficial and the degree to which it might be costly. Focal organizations might also be characterized in terms of whether their resources are used in organizations with which there is interaction, whether their members use the products of those organizations, whether their members are competitive with them, whether their members are dependent on them, and so on.

The most immediate environments for a focal organization are the organizations with which there is interaction. These organizations can be characterized by whether their members are dependent on or competitive with members of focal organizations, whether they supply resources to or take products from focal organizations, and the degree to which their members perceive interaction as beneficial or costly. Initially, the framework categorizes the variables as the following list indicates. Influences of variables in each category on variables in every other category would be looked for.

The researcher can start by assessing the differential impacts of multivariate sets of organizational and environmental characteristics on both quantity and quality of interaction. Statistical techniques are available to examine such differential impacts. Sub-

Environment

Other organization's
  members' dependency on
  focal organization
  members

Competitiveness of other
  organization's members
  with focal organization
  members

Supplier to focal
  organization

Perceived benefits of
  interaction with focal
  organization members

Perceived costs of interaction
  with focal organization
  members

Unit

Provider of resources
User of products
Degree of competition
Dependency on other
  organization
Perceived benefits of
  interaction
Perceived costs of interaction

Response

Amount of interaction
  with others
Cooperation in interaction
Conflict in interaction
Bargaining in interaction

sequently, however, the interaction itself may influence focal organizations or their environments (here other organizations, as determined by the research question). Results of the initial observations should help the researcher decide what kinds of changes might result from the interaction. He or she can then make statements about how long it should take before changes might be observable and can incorporate the intervals thus derived into later stages of the research.

For example, the researcher might find that a considerable amount of interaction between members of a focal organization and another organization reduces perceptions by people in one or both organizations about the degree to which the organizations are competitive and the degree to which interaction is costly. This finding suggests that amount of interaction reflects or causes the development of trust. Trust probably does not develop within a few days or weeks. The impact of interaction on feelings of trust among a substantial number of an organization's members probably takes at least months to occur. Another finding might be that cooperative interaction increases the degree to which products of focal organizations are used by members of other organizations but in no way changes the organizations along the other dimensions assessed. This change in product use may come about rather quickly and dramatically.

Certainly the implications of both initial studies that include simultaneously R's, U's, and E's and subsequent assessments examining how R's are translated into U's and E's can answer for us more-complex questions about organizational interactions and other issues than have been answered in the past. In fact, when the data are arrayed in this way, a large number of questions about organizational interactions suggest themselves and can be answered.

This example suggests a number of interesting and potentially serious problems with accepted research paradigms and practices in our field. As previously stated, if we assess unit and environmental characteristics at all, we normally assess them at the beginning of a study and assume that these assessments will remain valid for a long time. If responses have direct impacts on those characteristics, however, the characteristics will change. In fact, one might hypothesize that the more important a unit or environmental characteristic is in influencing responses of interest, the more likely it is to be influenced by those responses and to show substantial changes. Here we rely on notions drawn from open-system theory that suggest that if activity in one part of a system is directed to another part of the same system, then some energy from the latter part of the system might be directed back in a reciprocal manner.

Toward More-Integrative Research and Theory

If we were to do the things outlined in this chapter, how would our research and theory benefit? First, specifying variable sets related to general and enduring response tendencies and characteristics of responding units would suggest research designs and theories specifically stressing an examination of complex relations and a rejection of an emphasis on bivariate relations. We wish it were true that one sees few studies emphasizing bivariate analyses. It is not.

Our emphasis that organizations and groups do not behave may seem a minor point to many. If this emphasis reduces anthropomorphizing of organizations, however, it will have benefits. If we sharpen our thinking and hypothesizing and begin designing studies to test hypotheses about what individuals in positions of power in one organization form connections or make overtures to individuals in other organizations in order to reduce environmental uncertainty, we will have made considerable progress beyond what would be made testing vague hypotheses about connections between organizations during times of uncertainty. Such specific hypotheses, stressing the importance of individuals making the connections, would suggest that research and theory should include characteristics of these individuals as well as characteristics of the external environment and the organizations involved. In this regard we are in agreement with Katz and Kahn (1966), who reject the notion that organizations are living systems and agree that it is erroneous to apply to them organismic concepts that take interpretations far beyond the actual processes we study.

When we force our theories and empirical studies to be specific about our units of primary interest, we can be more precise about whether our operations are appropriate and are the best available ways to measure variables of interest. For example, which is a more accurate index of cohesion as a group-level response—number of intragroup contacts or a mean of affective responses reflecting satisfaction with one's co-workers obtained from a questionnaire? When authors specify units they are interested in, it will be easier to differentiate one person's response from another's environment. When this is done, we might be able to identify common linking pins across two or more independently developed pieces of research or theory. If research and theories can be placed within the confines of the framework developed in this chapter, simple as it is, integration becomes that much easier because consumers do not have to second-guess researchers and theorists about where their primary interests lie. We frequently see in both research and theory construction examples of indecision about primary units of interest. For example, too frequently inferences are drawn about individual responses based on data from the level of the school, school district, or community (see, for example, Bidwell and Kasarda, 1975; Coleman and others, 1966).

Application of this framework to any particular research effort offers another kind of benefit: it allows researchers to see obvious gaps in variables studied and possibilities for filling those gaps before an astute reviewer does so. Most members of journal editorial boards are all too familiar with completed research efforts in which results are potentially misleading because of failure to include in the research important variables known to covary significantly with one or more of the included variables.

Use of the extended framework should make it possible to separate more clearly than we usually do structural entities (for example, individuals, tasks) from processes (for example, the underlying constructs and logical processes detailed in Figure 1, Chapter One). Although systems theorists have opened our eyes more clearly than before to processes and although our theories deal predominantly with processes, our research focuses mainly on structure. We conclude that introducing time into our thinking about research design, while keeping structural entities separated from one another, is a step toward developing investigations that better uncover processes.

In sum, then, one purpose of the blueprint is to help us arrange variables in order to better understand mechanisms underlying response regularities. The extended framework should also help us address questions concerned with sources of activity that underlie responses. It will have the further purpose of helping researchers integrate existing research to find gaps in our knowledge. Finally, it should help organizational scientists coming from different backgrounds find their commonalities.

One might ask whether applying our suggestions to empirical efforts does not render them unjustifiably expensive. Applying one or a few of these points is not terribly expensive, except in that it requires researchers to think about what they need data about, based on theoretical considerations, before collecting data on everything only to find a relation between only two variables—and little conceptual rationale for that relation. It seems to us that research with high potential for producing misleading results, research that might be turned into expensive policy decisions that in the long run do not work, is more expensive (see, for example, Coleman and others, 1966).

CHAPTER 4

Aggregation Problems in Organizational Science

As Scott says (1975, p. 8), "Data collected over several decades suggest that on the average organizations are larger, more differentiated, and more bureaucratized than in the past." Paralleling that growth is a large increase in the number of people studying organizations. Frequently organizational scientists are accused of studying only the largest, most differentiated work organizations, organizations that account for only 9 percent of the work organizations in the United States. However, the overwhelming majority of the United States labor force is employed in these organizations. The facts that organizations are increasingly pervasive and that more attention is being devoted to studying them suggest that we must be sensitive simultaneously to various ways organizations interrelate and differentiate and to how people are tied together into work groups, departments, and organizations.

In Chapter Two we outlined some common paradigms that guide the content of organizational research and theory, locations in which observations are made, implicit boundaries set by researchers and theorists from one or another discipline, and kinds of inferences that researchers and theorists draw from their work. In Chapter Three we suggested a way results of our observations might be linked so that individuals will be more explicitly thought about in their organizational contexts and organizations will be more clearly seen as composed of individuals.

Until now we have carefully avoided a central problem concerned with the multiple views about the most appropriate way to analyze organizations—a problem that will become increasingly important as organizational scientists engage in research activities in which individuals, work groups, departments, and organizations are discussed explicitly and their characteristics are assessed simultaneously. This is the general problem of aggregation/disaggregation in organizational science.

A dictionary defintion of *aggregation* is "the action or process of collecting particles into a mass, or particulars into a whole; or of adding one particle to an amount; collection, assemblage, union" (*Compact Edition of the Oxford English Dictionary,* 1971). This definition says nothing about how the collection is made or about whether various aspects of the whole are homologous with other parts. Here we use the term *aggregation* in reference to the use of some combination of responses (R's) or unit characteristics (U's) to reflect something about the immediately more macro unit of analysis (E's). Equally common, we find aggregated data used to make inferences about R's at a more micro level of analysis, without disaggregation. *Disaggregation* refers to separation of the component particles within an aggregated mass or structure. In this chapter we focus mainly on aggregation problems as they occur in theory, in sampling, in introducing time dimensions into research, in measurement, in different approaches to data analysis, and in interpreting results.

A well-known example of an aggregation problem occurs in Durkheim's research on religion and suicide. Durkheim found that Catholic communities had lower suicide rates than Protestant communities. This finding may be interpreted in a number of ways, some explanations focusing on community characteristics and some on individual responses. Much depends on which unit of analysis is chosen.

In discussing the population ecology of organizations, Hannan and Freeman (1976, p. 933) make the following comment about aggregation: "Little attention is paid in the organizations literature to issues concerning proper units of analysis. . . . In fact, choice of unit is treated so casually as to suggest that is is not an issue. We suspect that the opposite is true—that the choice of unit involves subtle issues and has far-reaching consequences for research activity." Aggregation problems are not unique to our field. They abound across the physical and social sciences. Morgenstern (1963), in fact, discusses their abundance in economics. Many of the problems we discuss here arise simply from lack of clarity. Clarity about potential error introduced by aggregation might in itself result in introduction of fewer errors associated with different kinds of aggregation. In other instances real problems exist, and the simple plea for clarity will not cure them.

Should We Aggregate at All?

An initial problem is whether we should limit our research to responses and concepts clearly attached to the unit of interest (individuals, groups, or organizations). Much of our research involves aggregation of responses from a lower level to represent something more macro. For example, individual assessments of job satisfaction are often aggregated to represent group morale. It is possible, however, that group morale can be appropriately and unambiguously assessed only through observations uniquely tied to groups. Consequently, a sociometric technique to assess group cohesion (clearly a property of a group, not an individual) may provide a better measure of morale than aggregated satisfaction scores. From a theoretical viewpoint one can ask whether a concept developed to refer to individuals is equally applicable to higher-level units. For example, when we speak of decision making by individuals, groups, and organizations, do we mean the same thing for each unit? Or does *decision making* refer to one set of processes when applied to individuals and another set when applied to groups or to organizations?

These examples argue for the development of composition theories (specifying relations among forms of one construct represented at different levels of analysis) to supplement and enrich content theories (describing relations among distinct constructs within a single level of aggregation or across levels) and process theories (describing how different constructs are combined to produce response tendencies). These examples also pose an argument against aggregation. When composition theories are developed, some writers expect homology across levels of analysis. Thus, homology can be said to exist when, for example, the relation is the same between interpersonal communication and satisfaction measured at the individual level and intradepartmental information transmission and aggregate departmental satisfaction. Other writers, including Hannan (1971a), expect linkages among micro data to reflect different constructs than those same linkages generated from macro data in the same sample. The question is an empirical and a logical one. One could demonstrate homology or discontinuity of constructs empirically. One can also address this issue from a logical viewpoint. As we have seen throughout this book, it is difficult, if not impossible, to specify composition rules tying together dependent variables, even those that appear to reflect the same underlying processes. (As an example, see the discussion of turnover in Chapter One.) Given the difficulty in developing any composition rules, it may be unreasonable to expect those that will be developed to be homologous across conceptual levels. Identification of homologous linkages is probably less likely than is identification on nonhomologous linkages.

Two kinds of data are generally used to characterize groups and organizations: global data not divisible across individuals (such as organizational ownership) and aggregate data based on some composite of lower-level scores (such as mean job-satisfaction or median achievement scores). Global data are whole-unit data: each is a datum on the whole. When several global data are combined (regardless of how), we have aggregate data. Although both global and aggregate characteristics can be used to describe groups and organizations, the use of aggregate data and concepts makes it more likely that interpreters will be confused and information lost. A further disadvantage is that aggregate data are not directly linked to the level of aggregation about which inferences are made.

Aggregation from the individual to the group level creates ambiguity when group members are described as highly satisfied, quite married, and disproportionately educated. Use of aggregate data may obscure understanding when steps are not taken to determine whether a variable or construct has surplus meaning beyond that associated with its original level of assessment. Research on technology provides an example of the potential for information loss and data misinterpretation when aggregate data are used. A good deal of research on technology uses individuals' descriptions of the amount of standardization in tasks performed as an index of technology. Aggregate individual descriptors of task standardization are treated as characteristics of an organization's technology, based on the argument that measurement error and individual differences in perception average out to produce a more representative measure of technology than can be obtained by relying on one person's description of technology. When averaging individual perceptions to reduce measurement error, researchers class individual differences in perception with measurement error—that is, as sources of inaccuracy—although those differences may be due to task characteristics unique to an individual's position in the organization. Any aggregation that equates features unique to an individual's job with measurement error is based on assumptions with which we take exception. The product of such an aggregation cannot be interpreted unambiguously as an organizational characteristic. This kind of aggregation leads to another (and related) difficulty, loss of information. The simple majority of jobs in an organization may be highly automated, and the organization may therefore be characterized as "high technology." Yet thirty percent of the jobs may not be describable as high on automation. Thus, it is unlikely that individuals' task perceptions translate directly into organizational technology. Here homology cannot be assumed.

Individual perceptions of tasks as descriptors of some facet of technology do offer a useful means of unambiguously assessing at least one aspect of an organization: heterogeneity in individual perceptions of tasks in the organization. A measure of within-organization variance in perceptions of task characteristics provides an index of variability in task perceptions clearly tied to the organization rather than to the individual. This index may relate to characteristics of the organization with its members. Since a variance statistic can be linked clearly to an organization, it can be interpreted unambiguously as an organizational characteristic and has meaning different from that contained in individual-level responses. An example is Drexler's (1977) computation of within-organization homogeneity/heterogeneity on organizational climate. Drexler found that people in each organization tended to agree more in their descriptions of climate than people across organizations did; this small within-organization variance relative to between-organization variance suggests that averaged perceptions of climate might be a useful concept. Low variability in perceived climate is evidence supporting the contention that organizational characteristics are veridically assessed through individual perceptions.

Aggregate central tendency data, too, may provide useful information. Research on small-group processes suggests that group composition affects group performance. Findings indicate that two persons of low intelligence perform worse as a group than either of them performs working alone (Laughlin and Branch, 1972). Although aggregating intelligence across pairs of persons gives us the same ordering of persons as does looking at a frequency distribution of individual intelligence scores, the two measures are not related in the same way to performance. In this case, because homology does not exist, aggregation reveals the presence of an important effect, a different effect than one would infer if results were homologous across levels. Clearly, understanding social and organizational events requires theories of composition, describing relations across levels of analysis, as well as theories of content and process.

Since much aggregation is theoretically valuable, aggregation cannot be completely discouraged because of the ambiguity associated with its use. However, aggregation without specifying the rationale for it through theories of composition is the source of a good deal of confusion. Critiques of research on technology

(Lynch, 1974; Stanfield, 1976) attribute much of the lack of convergence in this area to conflicting operationalizations of the concept of technology. Sometimes technology is treated as a global or aggregate organizational characteristic, other times as an unaggregated individual-level variable. Virtually no study of technology specifies the rationale for the operationalizations used. Similarly, there is a growing concern in educational research with problems of interpretation brought about by using district or classroom data to predict what students will do. One should develop and apply global concepts and assessments to macrolevel, not microlevel, problems. If global concepts cannot be assessed globally, it may be acceptable to substitute aggregations. However, it is then incumbent on the researcher to explicate the relation between the aggregated data and the global concept. This activity ensures that attention is given this kind of relation and also directs explicit attention to choosing appropriate units of analysis in any research endeavor. Simply spelling out the nature of problems likely to occur through aggregation, a step toward developing increased sensitivity, is important if attention is ever to be directed to solving these problems.

Conceptual Aggregation

The first type of aggregation with which we will concern ourselves is conceptual, or theoretical, aggregation. This refers back to the discipline-oriented paradigms (discussed in Chapter Two) guiding our theory and research development based on those paradigms. Following is an example of a conceptual aggregation. To varying degrees people in organizations follow rules. Some of us might observe this response and develop theories of conformity to explain it. Theories of conformity are closely tied to observations of individual rule following. Observing the same response, others might develop the construct "formalization" and a more macro theory concerning how formalization develops. The theory is relatively distant from the observations. Clearly, conceptual aggregation is linked to levels of analysis associated with the various disciplines in organizational science. If the paradigm used to explain rule following emphasizes conceptualization and measurement at the organizational level, individual rule-following behavior is neatly dealt with by developing an organizational construct to describe that response in its aggregate form. It also follows that the level of aggregation at which a theory is developed influences aggregation issues concerned with sampling, time units, measurement, data-analysis and interpretation. Hence, various aggregation issues and potential problems they introduce are interdependent.

To clarify the role aggregation plays in organizational studies, we will have to rationalize more explicitly the conceptual aggregations we make. Only then will it be possible to evaluate the degree to which alternative conceptual and other kinds of aggregation are consonant with one another. Additionally, explicating the kinds of conceptual aggregations inherent in theories alerts us to potential points of misinterpretation. When level in theory is closely linked to level in observation, misinterpretation is less likely than when it is more distant. Clearly, dependent variables, or outcomes of interest, determine the level of aggregation at which theory is appropriately developed. One might ask whether constructs are "real" if they must be assessed with aggregated data. This question has been given insufficient attention.

From our discussions in Chapters Two and Three, it is apparent that the different conceptual aggregations characterizing several disciplines have led to problems in integrating research and theories. March and Olsen (1976) make the point that individuals' perceptions of organizations influence responses that in turn shape choices managers make regarding structure, technology, and responses to environments. When group and organizational characteristics are conceptualized as distinct from individual characteristics and responses, social phenomena focused on are viewed as a function of individual actions in a social context and are not thought to result from actions of isolated individuals.

Implicit in our conceptualizations of group and organizational characteristics and processes is the view of social collectives as nearly decomposable systems. Nearly decomposable systems are those in which interactions among the subsystems are weak but not negligible. In such systems the short-run responses of each component subsystem are approximately independent of the short-run responses of the other components, and in the long run, responses by any one component depend in only an aggregate way on responses of other components (Simon, 1969). In such systems "the whole is more than the sum of the parts, not in an ultimate, metaphysical sense, but in the important pragmatic sense that, given the properties of the parts and the laws of their interaction, it is not a trivial matter to infer the properties of the whole. In the face of complexity, an in-principle reductionist may be at the same time a pragmatic holist" (Simon, 1969, p. 86). Thus, a system is nearly decomposable if it can be subdivided and maintain the characteristics of the original system. If subdivision changes the system altogether, it is not decomposable. The system of Sears Roebuck stores exemplifies a nearly decomposable system. Although each store is a part of the Sears system, the stores function relatively independently, with only weak interactions. One Sears store is independent, in the short run, of what happens in other stores, and in any store activities are usually based only in an aggregate way on activities in other Sears stores. Thus, the stores can often be viewed independently of one another but have the system characteristics inherent in aggregation of Sears stores. If Sears stores were disaggregated and their members disperse (to be entrepreneurs, for example), the nature of the system would change.

Theory and research involving conceptual aggregations reflect this assessment of group and organizational characteristics as something different from the sum of the parts. At the same time, the concept of a nearly decomposable system is consistent with the development of rules for decomposition of organizational and group characteristics into their components. There is no reason aggregation and decomposition work cannot be conducted simultaneously if such work facilitates our development of composition theories as well as content theories.

Aggregation over Samples

As indicated previously, the appropriate unit to select for observation in any research program should be dictated by the units of theory. If one is interested, for example, in the impact of externally created stress on internal organizational interdependencies and in individual administrators' responses to stress in schools, one will not sample for observation total school districts. Individual schools and the people in them are more appropriate. Although this point appears logically straightforward, in fact there are numerous studies in which inferences are made about one level of analysis based on data from units at more macro levels. In discussing ecological correlations (in which, for example, aggregate data such as sex composition and average need for achievement are correlated across schools), Robinson (1950, pp. 351–352) notes: "In an ecological correlation the statistical object is a *group* of persons. . . . Ecological correlations are used in an impressive number of quantitative sociological studies some of which have now attained the status of classics. . . . In each study which uses ecological correlations, the obvious purpose is to discover something about the behavior of individuals. Ecological correlations are simply used because correlations between the properties of individuals are not available. In each instance, however, the substitution is made tacitly rather than explicitly." Robinson discusses the relation between an ecological and an individual correlation and shows that *there need be none.*

It is common for data to be aggregated across geographical areas because of the widespread use of census data. Pupils are nested in schools, employees in organizations, individuals in communities. Voters are nested in precincts, precincts in districts, and districts in counties. All of us are nested in numerous social or geographic groupings. Many times reliance on aggregated units of analysis is necessary because the areal unit is the unit of theory. For example, those of us interested in the influence of group composition on individual responses might well count the people in a group as an indication of group size. However, arbitrary partitioning into large aggregate units results in the use of units of analysis with no reference to the issue under study. One example is found in studies of community turnover rates, where rates are partially a function of chosen community boundaries, another in agricultural research in which yield per unit land area changes dramatically depending on how the researcher chooses or shifts areal boundaries. Choosing a unit of analysis without reference to the constructs under investigation is an unjustifiable expedient.

Areal units tend to flow into one another. Groups in organizations mingle; organizations often overlap with one another. Hannan (1971b) points out that most analysts are willing to assume that observations located close together in space and time are likely to be more alike than observations spaced more distantly. Cronbach (1976) calls for a model in which units are studied as they are embedded in other units. His thinking is reflected in our U and E notation in Chapter Three. However, Cronbach (1976, p. 1.24) states: "A model of units nested within larger units may be unrealistically simple even in schools. In simpler days, pupils were nested within classes, firms within industries, families within communities. Today, even a nine-year-old may work in a dozen groups and individual settings with several teachers and aides, all in the course of a school day. Similarly, the firm is often a conglomerate, and family members commute and so come under the influence of several communities."

Traditionally, organizational sociologists and organizational psychologists became involved in different kinds of sampling-aggregation problems. Sampling at a more macro level than one is really interested in making inferences about is a greater danger for sociologists than psychologists. However, those organizational social psychologists who work in laboratories contribute a different kind of sampling problem, one that results from differences between laboratory and field methods. In the laboratory one creates some conditions of an organization and watches its "members" respond. Serious time-aggregation problems are inherent in this approach. So are context problems, in that one creates an area while probably giving little thought to the degree to which the particular setting is found in real life. This problem is clearly associated with problems of generalizing laboratory results to organizations. In contrast, industrial-organizational psychologists and probably industrial engineers are usually interested in individuals, select them (or the man/machine interface) for study, make inferences about them, and ignore potential nesting effects. In fact, the common sampling problem contributed by these latter researchers is that they, for the most part, sample by convenience. Selection of samples is rarely based on units of theory.

Aggregation over Time

Aggregation over time is possibly the most important aggregation problem organizational scientists face. In most sciences events and processes have natural knowable cycles. Biologists, for example, develop theories consistent with life spans of organisms, physicists can assess the half-lives of atomic particles; these life spans guide theoretical development. When time spans for processes or events are obvious, they can be included in theorizing. Organizational scientists do not include in their conceptualizations notions about the way time mediates processes and responses, because they generally do not have natural cycles to guide them. For example, what is the half-life of an organization or a career? Does it differ across organizations, from one geographic area to another, from industry to industry, and so on?

In Chapter Three we stated that only when time is a part of our research designs is it possible to move from a static to a process view of organizations. However, time-series studies can generate results that are easily misinterpreted if the wrong time interval is chosen. The obvious problem is *how* to include time in our thinking. An initial step is for researchers to observe research sites closely before entering into full-scale time-series studies, in order to develop notions about what natural cycles of events relevant to dependent variables of interest operate in these sites. These naturally occurring benchmarks can then be used to help develop theories of composition that take time into account. For example, for someone doing research in schools, one natural time span is the school year. Even though it is arbitrarily determined, once implemented the school year and its divisions act as benchmarks and influence processes operating in schools. The school year can be included explicitly in some theories relevant to schools as organizations. Its inclusion should guide researchers in selecting appropriate time intervals at which to make observations. For the purposes of other research in schools, different intervals will be more appropriate. Reading skills, for example, might be expected to change directly after some intervention. In other organizations, ways to view time will usually be less obvious. In some it may be helpful to use production schedules to help establish benchmarks; in others (such as resorts) seasons may divide time more appropriately. Naturally occurring benchmarks, together with outcomes of interest and appropriate levels of analysis of theory guiding those outcomes, can be used to select appropriate time intervals for inclusion in research and theory construction. Failure to attend to time in developing theories and research strategies is seen across organizational science. It is probably most serious in laboratory research, in which we have no idea whether failure to establish realistic time intervals renders results useless.

The failure to take time into account seriously in our theories causes a number of problems in the way time is handled in research. At least three major problems in research are direct results of failure to specify the role time plays in our thinking about organizations. First, we often see data combined from samples collected at different times. Second, we see an increasing amount of research comparing measurements taken on the same variables at apparently arbitrary intervals. Third, we often see correlations between assessments of variables that reflect different units of time—for example, an assessment at a particular time of organizational climate over an unspecified time period and turnover in the same organization for the preceding two weeks.

As an example of the first kind of aggregation problem, consider a national probability sample. Suppose we are interested in learning about work experiences of minorities in a sample of United States workers. It is likely that any one sample will contain too few minority-group members to allow us to draw conclusions. To increase sample size, we can combine data from a series of samples over a number of years. However, a fuzzy time span will result. It will, of course, be unclear whether the resulting analyses reflect current or past minority work experience or—though, perhaps, bearing little relation to either—some combination of both. In such a case, a bootstrapping operation may be appropriate, in which similar trends in all samples are combined to form the basis for larger analyses, trends within samples being combined rather than combining samples and examining trends.

Almost unrelated is the second time problem, associated with increasing numbers of research programs using time-series designs (Cook and Campbell, 1976), in which the same variables are measured at different times. In a review of causal correlational techniques, Feldman (1975) discusses a number of cross-lagged correlational studies and notes that they use a wide range of time intervals. In none of the studies, however, is there mention of a theoretically specified causal interval; "Theoreticians seem to have neglected this aspect of causality, and the researcher is left to operate 'by guess and by God'" (p. 666). Our theories are insensitive to the natural cycles of individuals, groups, and organizations, and we have no ideas about proper intervals for aggregation over time. Thus, given their static nature, our theories fail to mirror the processes they attempt to describe and to indicate the measures that might operationalize processes.

The third way time is relevant to aggregation problems is more directly associated with measurement itself. Fuzziness regarding time intervals of variables results when data represent combinations of responses over some period of time. Measures of absenteeism or GPAs are common forms of aggregation over time. For example, data on absenteeism normally represent the number of absences over some period, ranging from one day to one year. The choice of the particular period over which absenteeism data are aggregated is seldom explained by the researcher. For data such as absenteeism or number of accidents, the underlying reason for aggregating is the low base rate of responses. On any given day in most organizations, most employees come to work and most do not have accidents. A measure of absenteeism based on a single day's attendance is unlikely to correlate with other variables of interest. We aggregate to increase the stability in our generalizations about something people do over time. Simultaneously we increase the variability that can be assessed in what a single person will do.

Another form of measurement across time occurs when data are collected through retrospection. When individuals are asked to recall behaviors or experiences, the events are generated before measurement. Whenever supervisors are asked to rate subordinates' performance over a specified or unspecified time period, both aggregation and retrospection problems result. Aggregation over time and retrospection measures both introduce ambiguity, because it becomes unclear when the response of interest occurred. When a time-aggregation datum is correlated with another measure, lack of synchronicity may result. Synchronicity, as described by Kenny (1975), means that two variables for which a correlation is calculated are measured for the same unit of time.

Coincidence between measures is important in interpreting

results of cross-lagged panel analyses. If a questionnaire is administered twice at a one-month interval and measures of satisfaction and motivation for each of those two times are derived from questionnaire responses, a significantly greater cross-lagged correlation between motivation at time 1 and satisfaction at time 2 than between motivation t_2 and satisfaction t_1 suggests that changes in motivation lead to changes in satisfaction (Figure 2). However, if absenteeism data are also collected for the month previous to each questionnaire administration and the relation of absenteeism to satisfaction is examined, a significantly greater correlation between satisfaction t_1 and absenteeism t_2 than between absenteeism t_1 and satisfaction t_2 is not readily interpretable as evidence of causation. The cross-lagged correlation for satisfaction t_1 and absenteeism t_2 is based on a time interval of one month or less; when satisfaction t_2 is correlated with absenteeism t_1, however, satisfaction is examined in relation to a measure of absenteeism based on individual responses beginning two months previously (Figure 3). Thus, satisfaction t_1 is

Figure 2. Cross-Lagged Panel Design with Synchronous Variables

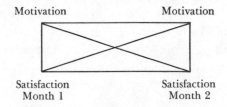

Motivation   Motivation

Satisfaction   Satisfaction
Month 1   Month 2

Figure 3. Cross-Lagged Panel Design with Nonsynchronous Variables

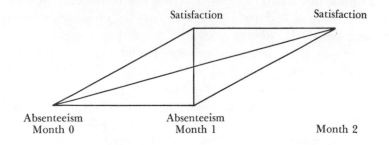

                    Satisfaction   Satisfaction

Absenteeism   Absenteeism
Month 0   Month 1   Month 2

correlated with a measure of absenteeism that is closer to it in time than is true for the other cross-lag. Since variables closer in time are likely to correlate more highly than variables measured further apart (Blalock, 1964; see also Chapter Five), in such a research design it would be difficult to conclude that satisfaction causes absenteeism. However, we might give credence to evidence suggesting that changes in absenteeism might lead to changes in satisfaction, because the time lag between absenteeism t_1 and satisfaction t_2 is longer than that associated with the other cross-lagged correlation.

For time-series analyses of other cross-lagged panel designs, the time intervals relevant to variables under study must likewise be taken into account in interpreting relations among variables. It is precarious to say that satisfaction influences performance when the performance takes place before the satisfaction is measured. Not unrelated are problems in interpretation that arise when the measures change or decay over time and hence are unstable or undependable.

Constraints on whom we can study and what we can measure will always result in some time-aggregation problems in research. We can, however, pay greater attention to the time problems inherent in our data and interpret our results in light of the implicit ambiguities resulting from differences in time spans. Attending explicitly to potential time problems will often make it possible to group samples more appropriately and select synchronous measures.

Aggregation over Measurements

In our discussion of time we mentioned problems that arise when variables assessed in the same study are not measured for the same time period. We also mentioned that interpretation problems occur when measures change over time. Here three additional aspects of measurement aggregation are discussed. One is the issue of "summary" variables, another is the issue of interaction variables, and a third, closely related issue is concerned with reciprocity among variables.

The first issue is closely related to our earlier discussions of concepts and processes, in which it became obvious that every assessment that can be made is the assessment of an outcome of some set of processes. For example, even when we write down someone's age, we have in front of us a summary of many things. A person's age indicates the amount of experiences that person has had. Figure 1 in Chapter One implies that observables are, in fact, summaries. For many variables we agree implicitly about the nature of the composite we observe; for some we need not worry about the composite. For example, the compositional effects resulting in a person's sex role identification are generally not of interest to organizational researchers. They are, however, of great interest to some biologists, physiologists, developmental psychologists, and other scientists. Too frequently researchers fail to address questions of composition relevant to complex observables nearer the center of theoretical interests in organizational science. This problem plagues research on organizational climate, and we see some investigations of climate that seemingly assess large components of job satisfaction, others that measure leadership attributes, and so on, equating these with climate. In research using the same constructs, there should be the same underlying meaning. Resolution about non-agreed-upon meaning is impossible until writers clearly explicate composition rules they think underlie their observations.

Another measurement-aggregation issue is an extension of the fact that observables are summaries. There are variables not easily attached to a particular unit of analysis. For example, job level and tenure are unique neither to individuals nor to organizations. They are variables that, whenever assessed, reflect interactions between things people do and aspects of their organizations. Although every assessment is a summary of something, some summaries are more easily tied to units of analysis than others are. Clarifying the degree to which a variable can be attached to a level of analysis helps researchers in two ways. First, it will become easier to assess variable sets for interdependence. For example, when we enter individual and organizational characteristics into the same research as independent variables, we probably think automatically of these two sets of characteristics as relatively independent of each other. Organization size (an organizational characteristic) and job tenure (an individual characteristic) are thought about as attached to different units of analysis. However, when one thinks of tenure as reflecting both what a person does and what happens to him or her in organizations, it becomes less obvious that tenure and personnel policies are as independent of each other as they may have appeared initially and more obvious that one should assess their independence before entering them into independent variable sets. Similarly, regrouping variables into categories of those closely tied to particular units of analysis (size) and those more clearly reflecting interaction (tenure) should help us choose data-analytic strategies. We can treat interactive variables in separate classes just as we do variables more clearly attached to individuals, groups, and organizations. Endler (1975) notes that the problem may be a pseudo one. Rather, we should be asking how individual differences and situations interact to evoke behavior.

Closely related to the nature of interaction of some variables and to their relative attachment to units of analysis is the fact that variables are causally interactive or reciprocal, a notion reflected in the temporal extension of our framework in Chapter Three. As James and others (1978, p. 21) point out in a discussion of research on psychological climate, "The underlying causal model of interactional psychology is, therefore, reciprocal causation, which is also referred to as 'transaction' (Pervin, 1968) and reciprocal interaction (Overton and Reese, 1973). This is not a new concept; nevertheless its ramifications appear only now to extend beyond theoretical treatments (Graen, 1976)." James and others discuss reciprocal causation between situational and individual measures. However, their notions can be extended to any set of variables. For example, organizational characteristics, such as structure and function, can influence each other. One change in a variable such as individual education level may lead to other changes in the same variable. James and others (1978, p. 27) state that "while psychologists have addressed the concept of reciprocal causation theoretically, research, including that in climate, has focused primarily on (implicit) unidirectional causal models or has simply avoided the issue of causality by emphasizing descriptive rather than causal interpretations of results; and . . . the ramifications of reciprocal causation for measurement, for interpreting what has been measured . . . and for the appropriateness of research design have not been recognized, resulting, in some instances, in the treatment of what appear to be pseudo issues."

New methodological models are clearly needed to take into account the summary nature of variables, their relative attachment to particular units of analysis, and their causal reciprocity. No entirely adequate solutions to the measurement problems introduced here have been developed.

Aggregation in Data Analysis

The majority of writings on aggregation focus on its effects on statistical analyses (Blalock, 1964; Hannan, 1971a; Hammond, 1973). Aggregation must be considered in interpreting results of data analyses because the way data are grouped may effect the values statistics take. The most commonly studied effect of aggregation is change in Pearson correlations and regression coefficients following shift in level of aggregation.

Blalock (1964) discusses the effect of four types of grouping on bivariate relations: random grouping, grouping that maximizes variation in the independent variable (x), grouping that maximizes variation in the dependent variable (y), and grouping by proximity (spatial or temporal). Although almost never used in organizational field research, random grouping is often discussed in comparison with other grouping strategies. If individuals are combined into groups randomly, there should be no relation between one group member's score and another's on any variable. For example, if we are interested in the relation between education (x) and income (y), and we randomly assign individuals to groups for which average education and income are calculated, the amount of education of one group member is in no way related to the amount of education of another. In this instance, the group or aggregate-level correlation and regression coefficients will be the same as those at the individual level. This is, of course, an artificial grouping strategy, since people are normally not grouped randomly. However, when we group by means other than random assignment, we run the risk of altering the values of statistics computed in data analysis.

One commonly used grouping strategy is the combination of individuals into larger units (groups) based on their scores on an independent variable, so as to maximize between-group variation in the independent variable. For example, in a study examining the relation of education (x) and income (y), census data may be used in which average income is presented for various education levels. As we know, income is influenced by education level and also by such things as economic conditions in a given locality. Computing mean income for each level of education (from grade school to postgraduate work) reduces the influence of "nuisance factors" such as economic conditions on income, where these nuisance factors represent causes of income that are independent of education. This reduction in the nuisance effect of other variables leads to an increased correlation between x and y, since x will explain a larger portion of the variation of y. The correlation coefficient (r_{xy}) increases as a function of the number of cases in each grouping. Thus, as we move from calculating average income for each year in school to calculating average income for those with a high school, college, or postgraduate education, the number of categories is reduced and the correlation coefficient increases.

Although the correlation coefficient is increased with this grouping strategy, the unstandardized regression coefficient (b_{yx}) remains constant across levels of aggregation. It has the same expected value at the aggregate level as at the individual level. As Hammond (1973) explains, we can think of a regression coefficient as defining a straight line through a scatter plot. We can construct a scatter plot of income against education by plotting a point for each individual or by plotting a point showing the mean income of each educational group. The points in the two plots will cluster around the same straight line, but in the second plot the points will be less widely dispersed. The regression coefficient (b_{yx}) remains the same, but the correlation changes. Consequently, if we are interested in drawing inferences about individual-level relations from aggregate data when grouping has been done according to the independent variable, we need to examine the regression coefficient of the dependent variable on the independent variable rather than the correlation among aggregate data.

There exists, however, one exception in which statistics based on data grouped on the independent variable cannot be interpreted at all. Hammond (1973) suggests that data aggregated on the independent variable can be interpreted only when no contextual effects exist. A contextual effect exists when the relation between variables is a function of the *level* of the independent vari able. The existence of such effects results in an aggregation bias that can change the correlation or regression coefficient or both. In discussing contextual effect, Hammond cites a problem surrounding the relation between race (x) and illiteracy (y) where race is dummy-coded. Correlations at the aggregate level are much higher than those at the individual level. If data are grouped geographically (as in census data), we expect that the aggregate correlation will be much larger than the individual correlation, because of uneven racial distribution in the United States. Geographical grouping is a form of grouping by the independent variable in this case, because geographical location and race are related. In this example, the regression of geographically aggregated data could be used to estimate the proportion of illiterates in each race if one could assume that rates of illiteracy do not vary systematically with racial composition of a given area. However, illiteracy rates historically have been higher in parts of the United States with the heaviest concentrations of blacks. A contextual effect exists, since the more blacks in an area, the greater the relation between race and illiteracy. In this case, neither the correlation nor the regression coefficient is interpretable. This example shows that we must consider plausible interaction effects before we interpret regression coefficients from data grouped on the independent variable.

When we group to maximize variation in the dependent variable, another aggregation problem arises. The correlation increases with grouping on the dependent variable, as does the regression coefficient b_{yx}. Such grouping makes these statistics uninterpretable, because maximizing variation in y confounds variation in y due to x with that due to other variables. In the case of the relation between education (x) and income (y), variation in income is a function of both education and economic conditions, among other variables. Maximizing variation in income (by calculating average education for each income level) confounds variation due to education with that due to economic conditions, and the effects of these variables on income cannot be isolated.

Effects of aggregation on either independent or dependent variables may be quite widespread. Consider the following example. We know that sex and education level are related. Let us assume that sex (independent variable) is directly related to education level (dependent variable) and that education affects one's ability to enter certain occupations. We may wish to relate sex and education using *data grouped by occupation.* If occupation segregation by sex is the result of differential education of men and women rather than the result of sex discrimination in professions, men and women in the same occupation will have the same average level of education. Those women who were able to obtain a higher education should have the same opportunity for employment as men with similar education have. In this instance, where a score on a dependent variable (education) leads to occupational entry, our data will show *no* relation between sex and education. Hence, the regression coefficient will be a biased estimate of individual-level relations. If, however, sex discrimination is the cause of differential occupational entry, data grouped by occupation will show a relation between sex and education, and the regression coefficient based on those data will provide an unbiased estimate of individual-level relations. The problem in using data such as these is not in aggregation itself but in the variables that influence the entry of individuals into groups.

The fourth grouping procedure is the most common in organizational research: grouping on the basis of the proximity of individuals (for example, by organization). Since most of the variables in which we are interested are likely to be found clustered to some degree, it is possible for the grouping criterion to produce a spurious relation between x and y. For example, we may find a high correlation between alienation and job routineness when aggregated to the organization or industry level but a far lower correlation at the individual level. This change in magnitude may be spurious and can be attributed to a shift in level of analysis. However, it is also possible that the degree of mechanization within each plant (a macrolevel variable) causes both alienation and routineness and is thereby responsible for their correlation. That the macro correlation is greater than the individual-level one may be a consequence of the impact of a more macro characteristic on individual responses. As Hannan (1971a) points out, all previous analyses of the ecological fallacy took the individual correlation as a pure datum to be used as a benchmark for comparison of aggregated effects. However, in organizational research variables from many levels of analysis may be relevant to the processes under study. Without theories addressing issues surrounding levels of analysis, we will have no way to know whether we have adequately specified the variables that influence the network of relations we find and no way to know whether effects resulting from shifting levels of analysis represent aggregation error or causal relations among variables.

Aggregations of Data and of Interpretations

Interpretation is usually the last step we perform in a particular conceptualization/data-gathering/analysis effort. Aggregation problems frequently occur at the interpretational level and are derived largely from what happened before. The absence of composition theories contributes to problems in interpreting relations among aggregate data. The most common interpretational errors are the fallacy of the wrong level and, especially, the ecological fallacy. "The 'fallacy of the wrong level' consists not in making inferences from one level of analysis to another, but in making direct *translation of properties or relations* from one level to another, that is, making too simple inferences. The fallacy can be committed working downward, by projecting from groups or categories to individuals, or upwards, by projecting from individuals to higher units. . . . The ecological fallacy in general consists in this: *properties found to be correlated at the higher level are assumed correlated, i.e., found within the same unit, at the lower level*" (Galtung, 1967, pp. 45–46). Hannan (1971a) notes other interpretational errors.

A classic example of wrong-level fallacies is in the possible interpretations of Durkheim's (1951) research on the relation of religion to suicide. In his analysis of the impact of religion on suicide (an individual-level response), Durkheim found that Catholic communities (characterized by large numbers of Catholics) had lower suicide rates (an aggregated variable) than Protestant communities. This finding may be the result of some property of Catholic communities, some characteristic of individual Catholics and Protestants, or an interaction between community composition and individual characteristics.

A series of interpretations is consistent with Durkheim's findings (Davis, 1961):

1. Catholics are less likely to commit suicide regardless of community religious composition.
2. Communities with Catholic majorities are characterized by low and equal suicide rates among both Catholics and Protestants.
3. Catholics are more likely to commit suicide than Protestants, but members of both religions are less likely to commit suicide in Catholic than Protestant communities.
4. In all communities the suicide rate for Catholics is the same, but the Protestant suicide rate declines with a high proportion of Catholics in the community.

All these conclusions suggest some relation between religion and suicide. They differ in their emphasis on social and individual factors because of assumptions made about the importance of each factor at the individual and group levels. Regardless of which, if any, of the conclusions is true, this example shows that a correlation between averages can tell us little about whether there is a group effect, an individual effect, or a group/individual interaction. Without data on the relation of individual-level suicide to religion, conclusions are difficult to draw.

A more recent example of the ecological fallacy is brought to our attention by Hannan, Freeman, and Meyer (1976), who critique a study by Bidwell and Kasarda (1975) that proposes a framework of analysis and a way of thinking about school effectiveness. The Bidwell and Kasarda model contains a number of organizational structural characteristics and discusses their impact on school effectiveness. Hannan, Freeman, and Meyer criticize Bidwell and Kasarda for making the logical leap of drawing inferences about individuals based on school-district data. They cite the following from Bidwell and Kasarda (1975, p. 63): "In the usual classroom pupil-teacher interaction is dyadic. If we assume that student achievement is some positive function of the rates of such interaction, then the more pupils per teacher the lower the aggregate level of achievement." Hannan, Freeman, and Meyer (1976, p. 138) say: "This statement contains an unannounced shift in level of analysis in its last clause which moves to the aggregate level. But clearly the theoretical argument concerns the experience of individual students, not aggregates of students. Why not, then, study achievement at the individual level? The authors take pains to point out that they are not conducting a study of the determinants of individual achievement."

In addressing their critics, Bidwell and Kasarda (1976, pp. 152–153) state: "According to [Hannan, Freeman, and Meyer], because a portion of our theoretical argument was couched at the level of individual events, our model and data analysis also should have been at the individual level. . . . In fact, it is entirely appropriate to advance ecological propositions and assess them with ecological variables, yet to ground these propositions on a theory in which individual events serve as mechanisms."

Clearly, we take issue with Bidwell and Kasarda. Just as clearly, others do not see problems that occur when errors of specification are made.

Another interpretational aggregation problem important to organizational scientists is the violation of weak stochastic transitivity. Take as an example three idealized individuals who represent a market and state their preferences for goods x, y, and z as shown in Table 2.

Note that for each person there is perfect transitivity. However, when we aggregate individual scores to the group (market) level, we find that $P(x>y) = 2/3$, $P(y>z) = 2/3$, but $P(x>z) = 1/3$, violating weak stochastic transitivity. Students of consumer behavior frequently aggregate information about responses by individual buyers as indicators of the popularity of some product. In our example the market responds irrationally but each person in the market is rational.

Table 2. Preferences of Three Individuals for Three Goods x, y, z

Individuals	Preferences			
1	$x>y$	$y>z$	$x>z$	$x>y>z$
2	$x>y$	$z>y$	$z>x$	$z>x>y$
3	$y>x$	$y>z$	$z>x$	$y>z>x$

Table 3. Rank Orders of Preferences for Compact Models

Individuals	Aardvark	Bull	Crocodile	Dachshund
A	1	2	3	4
B	3	2	4	1
C	4	2	1	3

As another example, a marketing executive for an automobile manufacturer is considering which of the manufacturer's four compact automobiles to emphasize in sales and production. Data from three types of consumers, whose preferences Table 3 shows, are used to draw reference about the popularity of different compact models. The Aardvark, Crocodile, and Dachshund each have an average rank performance of 2-2/3. Because the Bull has a better average popularity rating, 2.0, than any of the other three compacts, its production is emphasized. Yet, if the other three automobiles were also manufactured, the Bull would never be purchased. Inferences drawn from aggregate data can be incorrect about what people prefer because they fail to take into account systematic order preferences that people may have.

Interpretational aggregation problems are probably easiest to rectify; it is fairly easy to assess similarity between the level of interpretation and the level at which data were gathered. As is obvious from the examples presented, generalizing inferences made about relations found at one level to another level of analysis is risky at best.

Assignment of Macro-Level Scores to Individuals

Assigning individuals macro-level scores—scores associated with groups or organizations—is based on the same assumption as aggregation is: that individuals in a given unit or collective are homogeneous with respect to a particular variable. In contrast to situations in which data are aggregated to reflect more macro characteristics or responses, situations in which macro scores are available usually provide no way to assess individual homogeneity on the variable of interest. For example, individuals in a production department are assigned the department's score on a measure of automation, but some of them work on less automated equipment than others. If an individual-level measure of automation were created, department scores could be supplemented with information on the type of equipment each person uses. Homogeneity would then be testable.

Not all group-level scores are amenable to individual operationalization. Size, for example, cannot be broken down readily into individual-level variables. If the group-level variable is based on some combination of individual attributes used to form counts or ratios, homogeneity is not an issue.

Assignment of higher-level scores to individuals can be useful in understanding individual-level responses. The sex composition of a group is an example of a case in which a group-level variable (sex ratio) could be related to an individual response. However, a group-level variable may not mean the same thing to all people in the group. In a group composed of five women and one man, the sex ratio is 5:6. The lone male, however, may perceive the group as being all female. Thus, individual-level perceptions of higher-level variables are often important to understanding relations among cross-level variables. Even when homogeneity is not a problem, individual-level measures that parallel higher-level variables are relevant to understanding the impact of group characteristics on individual responses.

Disaggregation

Disaggregation, earlier defined as the separation of component particles of an aggregated mass or structure, does not appear to pose the same problems as aggregation does. We will briefly mention each category of aggregation discussed here with a view to how disaggregation might apply.

The problem of disaggregating *units of theory* would have to do with applying to micro units of analysis theories developed on more macro units. This is rarely, if ever, done in the social sciences. One is not likely to see a model of formal organization applied to people. But one is likely to see statements about organizations as analogous to people: for example, that organizations "behave."

Disaggregation over *time* poses the same problems as aggregation. At the risk of repetition, we must say that only inclusion of time in our theories can rectify problems detailed here.

It is clearly possible and often probable that a researcher will sample from a level or use *measurements* representing a level that is inconsistent with the level of theory guiding the research. In such cases more refined data are collected than are needed to answer a question, or irrelevant data are generated. As Barton (1968, p. 1) notes in his perhaps overzealous criticism of survey research, "For the last thirty years, empirical social science research has been dominated by the sample survey. But as usually practiced using random sampling of individuals, the survey is a sociological meat-grinder, tearing the individual from his social context and guaranteeing that nobody in the study interacts with anyone else in it. It is a little like a biologist putting his experimental animals through a hamburger machine and looking at every hundredth cell through a microscope; anatomy and physiology get lost, structure and function disappear, and one is left with cell biology." More commonly, disaggregated data are unavailable and researchers rely, as previously discussed, on aggregate data in making inferences about more micro relations. In large-scale research the expense of keeping more than summary information and the generally limited utility of the additional information often militate against its availability (Hedrick, Boruch, and Ross, in press). As indicated before, this lack of information does not offer researchers an excuse for making errors of specification—that is, translating properties or relations directly from one level to another, usually from higher to lower.

The potential problems of disaggregation in *data analysis* are so closely tied with problems of disaggregation in measurement that they hardly deserve separate discussion. The analytic techniques one uses are necessarily closely associated with the measures one chooses. When they are not consistent with those measures, the analytic results should be nonsensical enough to alert researchers to re-evaluate their analytic techniques.

Interpretational disaggregation probably cannot occur. The usual problem involved in making specification errors is that one cannot disaggregate because the data with which to do so do not exist.

In this chapter, we have addressed problems that occur when aggregation is not explicitly thought about in theorizing and in research. We pose no solutions except clarity in analytic thinking. At this time one can only say that the potential impact of aggregation on research and theory must be addressed before solutions can be developed. Theories of composition are needed to augment content and process theories in organizational science. Aggregation problems will not disappear simply because we are unwilling to face them.

CHAPTER 5

✻ ✻ ✻ ✻ ✻ ✻ ✻

Staffing and Maintaining Organizations

✻ ✻ ✻ ✻ ✻ ✻ ✻ ✻ ✻ ✻ ✻ ✻ ✻ ✻

In this chapter we will examine approaches taken by organizational researchers to studying two distinct problems in organizations. The first, the problem of selecting people into organizations, has been the province of industrial psychologists with their decidedly microlevel, individual-differences approach to studying responses. It could be argued that this is the oldest research problem facing persons who must staff organizations. One can even find a reference to it in Judges 7:4–7, where the Lord outlines for Gideon a one-item selection test for staffing an army. The Lord explained to Gideon that his army, several thousand strong, was too large. After removing the self-proclaimed fearful and afraid from the thirty and two thousand, Gideon was left with ten thousand, which the

Lord still considered too large. He therefore told Gideon to have the army drink from a nearby body of water. Those who lapped from the water with their tongues like dogs and those who knelt to drink were sent home. The three hundred who cupped water in their hands and brought it to their mouths were retained for the expeditionary force. Although the Lord does not explain the rationale of his test to Gideon, the test has been interpreted as a method of screening out those who would expose their backs to the enemy while drinking and of retaining those who would be more cautious. Empirical evidence that would establish the validity of this single-item selection test to the satisfaction of an Equal Employment Opportunity Commission examiner was not provided.

The second problem is that of keeping people in organizations once they are selected. This is the problem of attrition, or turnover. This problem has been researched and theorized about by individuals representing the most micro to the most macro orientations: Industrial-organizational psychologists typically study decisions made by individual workers to terminate their employment with a particular company. Economists and sociologists frequently aggregate turnover statistics (usually expressed as voluntary terminations per 1,000 workers in the civilian work force) to the level of industries and even entire nations.

Our major purposes in writing this chapter are to explicate the nature of past research done in these areas and to show some major deficiencies. These deficiencies are caused by discipline-induced myopia that results in a failure for those of us in one discipline to be attentive to potential influences on responses caused by characteristics other than the ones shown important in our favorite research and theories. A final purpose is to show how these research areas might be developed more completely in the future.

Selection Research

Selection research in organizational science has been popular for more than sixty years. Research by sociologists on the certification process might reasonably be considered selection research viewed from a macro-orientation. However, the focus of most of this research is not on organizational entry but on the social dynamics of the process. Although this research is tangentially related to selection research, we will not review it here. Interest by psychologists in selection has been intense during three periods: 1914–1918, 1942–1945, and 1970 to the present. The first two periods of high activity were stimulated by our national need to select qualified military personnel during World Wars I and II. The present activity has its roots in Title VII of the 1964 Civil Rights Act. It is worth noting that the crash programs of 1918 and 1942 yielded impressive results compared with what would have been achieved using random selection methods.

The unfortunate and discouraging state of the art in selection research and practice is conveyed by two reviews of the literature. Between 1928, when Hull surveyed the literature, and 1966, when the accumulated literature was again surveyed by Ghiselli, no progress had occurred (see Hull, 1928; Ghiselli, 1966). This lack of progress was noted in all areas related to selection and placement: levels of empirically established validities, major theoretical development, innovations in paradigms, and development of more appropriate modes of task and worker characteristics.

Figure 4 speaks to the state of the art in selection research. This figure is anything but hypothetical. The curve is a smoothed version of a curve that would be generated if one were to summarize the literature on the relation between predictor and criterion in selection research as a function of the interval between measurements. The initial relation of about .30 quickly drops to zero and remains there over time. The relation is so nearly ubiquitous that the same function can be observed over the entire career of a manager or even over as short a period as an hour in a laboratory study of performance on a modified Mashburn apparatus (a device designed to tap skills similar to those used in flying an airplane equipped with a joy stick and rudder bar). The curve tells us that as individuals accumulate experience at tasks, initial validities of predictors drop to zero. This fact might suggest that some fallacious assumptions underlie selection research. It is certainly true that the *lack* of a relation between predictor and criterion is more permanent than their fleeting initial relation.

The initial level of the relation, the gradient of the slope, and the asymptote are all complex functions of a large number of

Figure 4. Expected Relation Between Predictor Information and
Criterion (Performance) as a Function of Time: The Vanishing Validity
Coefficient.

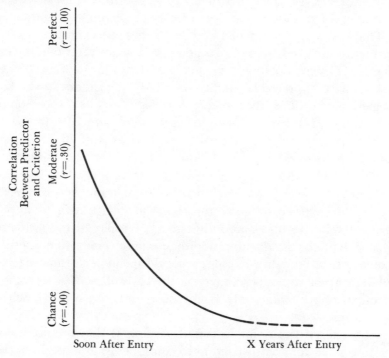

factors, including kinds of predictor information used, kinds of
criterion information obtained, time intervals, situational characteristics, reliabilities of measures, restriction of ranges, and sample
sizes. These factors can operate to change all the parameters of the
curve. However, the same general finding will nearly always appear, even if one uses initial level of performance on the task or
job, rather than some ability measure, as a predictor of later performance (Alvares and Hulin, 1972, 1973; Dunham, 1974;
Humphreys, 1962). Further, the more steps that intervene between
the actual responses and the evaluation of the responses, the more
likely the gradient is to be flatter and the asymptote higher. This
probably says more about bias, halo, and attributed stability of performance in ratings than it does about predictor/performance
relations.

We hasten to add that the rather dramatic decrease in size of validity coefficients as a function of time does not speak to the utility of the selection instrument in question as contrasted with the utility of a random selection process. For example, Humphreys (1968) empirically demonstrated and commented on the fleeting nature of the prediction of college success. American College Testing (ACT) scores obtained during a student's junior year in high school have appreciable validity for predicting grades in the first semester of college. By the eighth college semester, the relation between ACT scores (assessed in high school) and GPA has dropped to nearly zero. This drop is not an artifact of increasing homogeneity and restriction of range, since Humphreys included only students who completed all eight semesters of college. We reiterate, however, that the drop in correlation between ACT scores and semester-by-semester grades in college from an appreciable level to zero says nothing about the utility of the test compared with the utility of random selection. The latter question could be answered only by comparing the mean performance levels of a group of students selected on the basis of ACT scores and a group admitted randomly from the population of high school graduates.

The crucial point in this discussion is that organizational scientists are apparently content to continue using implicit models of individuals and explicit paradigms for conducting selection studies that consistently yield data suggesting our goals are shortsighted; we are willing to accept short-term prediction in the absence of long-term prediction, and we do little to modify either our paradigms or our models of individuals. It perhaps should be pointed out that selection research shows much the same dismal pattern of results that one finds in the prediction of other performance, general adjustment, adjustment to society (as in studies of delinquency), responses to treatments (as in education or psychotherapy), responses to parole, or treatment for alcoholism. Thus, this is not a problem unique to organizational research.

Findings such as those just discussed are both important and discouraging enough that we should examine the procedures used in selection research to gain some insights into possible causes of vanishing validity of coefficients. The kinds and amounts of pre-

Figure 5. The Analytic Approach

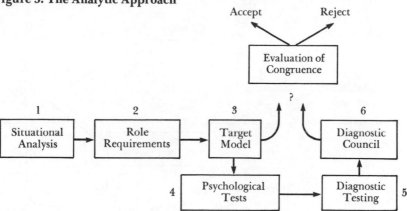

Source: Wiggins (1973, p. 457).

liminary research work done before any test battery is put into use vary considerably. Stern, Stein, and Bloom (1956) discuss in detail three prototypical approaches that have been used in preliminary phases of research. The first, outlined in Figure 5, they call the analytic approach. In this approach investigators engage in extensive analyses of situational constraints and variables (including identification, location, criterion standards, and biases of significant others) and role requirements. They then construct target models before tests are selected and used. After construction of target models and selection of tests, the tests are empirically validated to determine the extent of their relations to job performance. Tests that do not withstand the scrutiny of the validation procedure are eliminated or changed; possibly, even, new target models are constructed. Iterations to an accurate target model and appropriate assessments of the model based on successive approximations should be more often expected than accurate models derived from initial study.

At the other extreme is the empirical approach, diagrammed in Figure 6. In this procedure, an investigator first determines standards of performance. Individuals already on the job are then classified on the basis of these performance standards into two categories: those considered successful and those not considered successful. Tests thought to be related to performance standards are administered to these groups of individuals, and differ-

Figure 6. The Empirical Approach

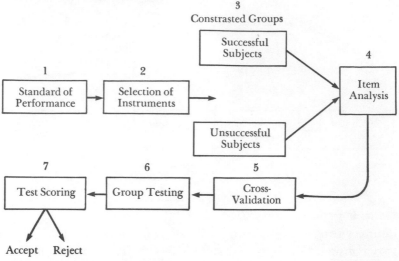

Source: *Wiggins (1973, p. 468).*

ences on resulting scores are examined. These tests often must be refined and item analyses done in order to select the best items from among those making up the item or test pool. The tests are cross-validated by administering the newly developed tests and applying previously developed methods of combining test results into overall predictions. The empirical validity of the tests is defined as the predictive ability of the test batteries on these new individuals.

The empirical approach to selection research is based on an incorrect syllogism. The assumption is made that, for example, if all successful individuals are found to be highly intelligent and an applicant is intelligent, the applicant will be successful. This is identical to the reasoning that says "All A are B. This person is B. Therefore this person will be (or is) A." The statement "All A are B" does not imply "All B are A." This fallacy alone might account for the discouraging results whenever test batteries developed on present organization members are put into use in predicting success or failure of future members.

The two approaches to selection just presented represent the extremes of the "analytical to empirical" continuum. In practice something somewhere in between is usually done, as shown in Figure 7. In this diagram, a number of steps in the analytic approach

Figure 7. The Synthetic Approach

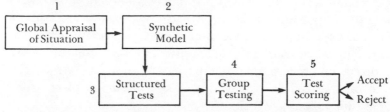

Source: Wiggins (1973, p. 468).

are short-circuited in an attempt at maximizing economy and shortening time intervals between initiating research and putting tests into use as selection devices.

Regardless of whether one uses the analytic or the empirical approach, the end results of the research and the underlying logic are the same. An applicant's test scores are compared with scores obtained by a group of individuals thought to be successful. An applicant who resembles the successful group is hired. An applicant who resembles the unsuccessful group is not hired. Cutoff points between success and nonsuccess are often arbitrarily determined. Whatever approaches are taken, *the tests must be validated against job-related criteria.* The ability to predict job-related criteria is the goal of all selection research, but it took Title VII of the 1964 Civil Rights Act, a Supreme Court decision (*Griggs* v. *Duke Power,* 1971), and the Equal Employment Opportunity Commission to drive the point home to American business organizations. The necessity for empirical validation of selection devices does mean that whatever approach one takes to selection studies, in the end they are all judged by the extent to which they can be used to predict relevant criteria.

An important factor here is the federal government's intervention in test research. The "guidelines" developed as a result of case law and public pressure for research in this area specify what is acceptable scientific research. Once these "guidelines" achieve the force of law, they will be chiseled into stone, and changes in paradigms or procedures will be achieved only after considerable difficulty and harassment. At the moment, test-validation procedures, tests in use, criteria for performance, and obtained reliabilities and validities are all subject to scrutiny in the courts.

Whether the courts are reasonable locations for deciding matters of science and technology is, unfortunately, a question we no longer have the opportunity to answer. Scrutiny, however, has had the effect of exposing many defects in current selection practices. The disturbingly low validities characteristic of research in this area are made even more apparent, and public attention is now focused on what can best be described as a dreary collection of statistically significant validity coefficients.

Organizational scientists engaged in personnel-selection research are responsive to both low levels of predictability of behavior by means of psychological tests and our lack of progress over the span of sixty years. Numerous suggestions are offered as panaceas. New lines of research and new approaches have been taken. Most of these approaches are little more than minor tinkerings with elements of the basic selection paradigm; few attempt dramatic change in the paradigm itself.

New approaches often take the form of more extensive criterion assessments, developments of taxonomies of human abilities and personalities, procedures to deal with the way information is combined into predictive equations, attempts to predict errors of prediction, global assessments of "whole" individuals rather than of isolated characteristics, quantifications of utilities of selection procedures, use of clinical rather than statistical prediction procedures, and use of statistical rather than clinical prediction procedures.

These new approaches have a cyclical nature. Every few years our attention moves from one new approach to a different new approach under a different (and new) label. All too frequently our newest development had been tried and abandoned several years before because promised results were honored more in the promise than in the keeping. Whatever approach is in vogue, it is normally fitted out with more elaborate statistical procedures than those preceding it, and results are produced that initially appear to justify the use of the new methods. Unfortunately, the next wave of research frequently indicates that the clothing of the new emperor is just as transparent as that of the previous one, and in fact, when we view him without our distorting prisms, we must conclude that he is just as naked as his predecessor was.

Some examples will illustrate the periodic "new" developments. Shortly after World War II we saw the development of forced-choice rating scales designed to counteract raters' unfortunate tendencies to rate all ratees superior or at least above average. The logic behind forced-choice rating scales is straightforward. If we can somehow force raters to choose from among a set of adjectives those most descriptive of the ratee while not informing raters which adjectives discriminate between successful and unsuccessful performers, we can obtain a more valid indication of ratee performance. Unfortunately, raters do not like being tricked, and with a little ingenuity, most are able to defeat the system. Distributions of assigned ratings are not markedly improved.

When this approach failed to live up to expectations, we turned to a rating procedure designed to help raters and provide them with as much information as possible, rather than withholding information and tricking them. This procedure also allowed them to make descriptive, rather than evaluative, statements. The best example of this newer approach is supplied by Smith and Kendall (1963), who present in detail their rationale for the development of behaviorally anchored rating scales. It is obviously too early to make any judgments about the utility of this scale format, but accumulating evidence suggests that the gains are marginal, especially when the amount of work necessary to generate the scales is considered.

Periodically we see attempts to avoid ratings made by fallible and probably biased observers as measures of performance and to substitute objective, performance-based measures. Unfortunately, performance in organizations is usually far too complex to be summarized in a single measure (even where such a measure exists). A weighted combination of individual elements resulting in one performance dimension must be generated if complex criteria are to be useful in an applied selection program. Even though weighting attempts probably reflect the complexity of performance in organizations, they have proved extremely difficult to handle statistically—where they are possible to implement. Applying them to incumbents in work roles where there is no objective output is virtually impossible.

Efforts to tinker with predictor information have been equally persistent. Currently we see a rebirth of assessment centers patterned after the World War II Office of Strategic Services assessment center established to select spies (U.S. Office of Strategic Services Assessment Staff, 1948). Unfortunately, the effectiveness of the assessment center in selecting spies from among applicants was never empirically demonstrated. Increases in validity of selection above conventional procedures (where increases exist at all) seem hardly worth the efforts and costs of assessment centers. Similarly, we have seen attempts to move away from conventional measures of ability toward assessments of needs, drives, and personality characteristics. These attempts were born, passed from the scene, and are occasionally reborn because of our discouragement with the status quo.

There have also been attempts to change the way we combine predictor information into an overall indication of the expected level of performance by an applicant. Normally, where assessments are made of a number of individual characteristics thought to be related to success, these multiple assessments are weighted according to their relation with a criterion and are combined into an overall prediction. Such procedures are often very effective in reducing prediction errors in the sample on which the weights are developed. Results are notoriously unstable, however, when applied to a different sample of workers from a different organization or even when applied to a different sample of workers from the same organization. This instability has led to attempts to develop procedures that are more stable and are more likely to generalize to other samples and situations.

In addition, the logic of additively combining predictor information into a weighted combination has been questioned. Suppose, for example, that, stimulated by the obvious adverse impact on blacks of the present procedures for selecting tenors for a national opera company, one wanted to develop a new selection procedure. A careful task analysis might suggest that important characteristics are quality of voice, pitch discrimination, acting ability, appropriate voice range, and some knowledge of Italian, French, and German. Obviously no amount of voice quality, pitch discrimination, or acting ability can compensate for inability to sing above middle C. Conversely, a total lack of pitch discrimination cannot be compensated for by any combination of the other qualities. Surplus amounts of one characteristic cannot compensate for failing in other areas. Applicants must be judged on each of the desired attributes independently. In this case we would very likely adopt a multiple-cutoff approach to selection and establish a minimum amount of each characteristic that must be possessed by every applicant before admission to the opera troupe.

Such disjunctive selection procedures have proved no better than the procedures they were designed to replace, probably because most human abilities are positively related to one another; individuals who have large amounts of one ability tend to have large amounts of other abilities, and the two procedures end up selecting nearly the same applicants. Further, with unreliable predictors, the reliability of the decisions is very low, lower than that of decisions based on a compensatory model.

Despite the long history of selection research, one would have to be extraordinarily optimistic to see any appreciable progress in our understanding over the years. We have deliberately painted a gloomy picture of the state of the art, perhaps an overly pessimistic one. When costs and savings are computed, validity coefficients of .30 have possible substantial utility, despite statements to the contrary. Claims for positive utility have tended to lead us to accept low predictability as inevitable and to expend our efforts justifying our product rather than improving it. Doing that leads to further inability of organizational sciences in general, and personnel-policy research in particular, to influence public policy.

But why the dreary state of the art? It is possible that most selection studies and programs make at least two implicit and potentially false assumptions. The first is that environmental characteristics (E's) do not interact with individual differences (U's) to produce responses (R's) of interest. Yet there is evidence that in other areas they do (Ekehammar, 1974; Mischel, 1973). And we know of no investigations in selection done to assess this assumption. Responses are assumed to be a result of individual differences. Accordingly, if scores on the Wonderlic Personnel Test are related to performance for workers in some sample, then the test is used for selection regardless of supervisor differences, task demands, or group composition.

The second assumption is that experience in an organization has no systematic effects on the members of the organization in terms of characteristics on which selection is based. Assessments of characteristics before organizational entry are assumed to remain valid and accurate descriptions of individuals over long periods, possibly spanning years, in a complex organizational environment. Figure 4 gives us a hint that they may not remain so. In addition, research by Alvares and Hulin (1973) and Dunham (1974) provides empirical testimony to the falsity of the assumption.

Selection from an Interactionist Viewpoint

Lest we mislead readers into thinking we are about to offer a radically new paradigm, we hasten to note that our approach, though more than a minor tinkering, is less than a truly radical change. Here we will place selection research and practice within the context of the framework developed in Chapter Three. Our suggestions for new approaches are consistent with the ideas contained in our framework and with the accumulated empirical literature relevant to individuals, environments, and responses.

Our first recommendation is straightforward and can be easily predicted. Much work has gone into developing standardized measures of individual differences—that is, taxonomies of individual characteristics thought to be related to important responses—and criterion assessments. These two lines of research stand in sharp contrast to the work *not* done in conceptualizing and developing *response-relevant*, objective dimensions of environments (or organizations) and relating these dimensions to individual characteristics and responses. We are not overlooking the work of Schneider (1975) on perceived organizational climate. Our concern is that perceived dimensions of organizational climate may contain unwanted variance that in turn may generate spurious response/response relations. Nor are we overlooking the work of Pugh and his associates (see, for example, Pugh and others, 1968a and b). Our concern with Pugh's taxonomic approach to discovering relevant dimensions of organizations is that the dimensions discovered do not appear related in any substantial way to relevant responses made by members of organizations. In support of Pugh's work, it is possible that organizational characteristics do not directly influence individual responses but that these influences are mediated by intraorganizational phenomena. For example, in a now-classic literature review, Porter and Lawler (1965) state that organization size is not directly related to individual job satisfaction but that subgroup size is. Organization size probably influences subgroup size, which in turn influences job satisfaction, which may in turn influence organization size. If size influences exist, they may be uniform or discontinuous across organizations and their subunits. A number of empirical and theoretical questions are generated here. Their answers rest on future development of composition theories; consideration of variables as interactive and reciprocal; empirical research in which observations are made simultaneously of individual responses, group characteristics, and organizational characteristics; and the use of these observations to identify processes by which influences operate. Here we reiterate a point made earlier. Conceptual and developmental work on individual differences (U's), criterion assessments (R's), or taxonomies of organizations (E's) without a simultaneous consideration of the other two variable sets is sterile and will likely generate sets of concepts or measures with little relevance to responses made by individuals in complex situations.

This first recommendation follows directly from our position that responses are best understood as functions of characteristics of responding units (in this case individuals) and environments within which responses occur. We are likely to observe both direct and interactive relations among characteristics of environments and characteristics of individuals in producing responses. This point cannot be overstressed, since much of the slowly accumulating literature in organizational research suggests that characteristics of intraorganizational environments account for a greater portion of responses by people than individual differences do. Without adequate conceptualization and assessments of response-relevant environmental characteristics in selection studies, influences of these characteristics must be assigned to the category of errors of prediction. Such assignment has the inevitable result of reducing the apparent predictability of performance. This recommendation is closely related to portions of a model of selection (Dunnette, 1966). It is hoped that one more statement about the importance of situational characteristics in selection research will lead to more frequent examples of concern put into practice rather than concern expressed and then ignored.

A second recommendation is that researchers recognize that environmental characteristics directly influence characteristics of people who work (or exist) in particular situations. This fact suggests that individual characteristics (Us) assessed before organizational entry may be only indirectly related to the same characteristics assessed in the same individuals after experience in an organization. This hypothesis further suggests that we must build into selection procedures mechanisms for examining direct influences of environments on individuals' characteristics, particularly those characteristics relevant to performance. The result should be a procedure explicitly attempting to counteract the unfortunate tendency of validity coefficients to decline inexorably toward zero over time.

One way to generate such a procedure is to consider dynamic models that make explicit the lawful changes in individuals as a function of environmental characteristics. In selection research this might lead to using individual characteristics in combination with situational characteristics to predict two things. The first is the traditional expected level of initial performance (which is really all we can predict now). The other is the expected value of individual characteristics after a period of exposure to a given environment. The assumption is that although all individuals will exhibit some change, some individuals will change more than others in predicted directions. Using such a dynamic model, one might make substantially different predictions about initial levels of performance and expected levels of performance after exposure to the environment created by the organization. Selection decisions would involve consideration of both predictions.

We must also recognize that individuals alter and restructure tasks and situations to fit their abilities and personalities. Although we naively think we select individuals to perform a particular task, after a short time some jobs resemble only slightly what they were initially.

Last, we must recognize the direct influences of situational characteristics on relations between *responses* and job *performance as assessed.* On many jobs, environmental characteristics strongly influence the effectiveness of individuals' responses. We can probably predict responses, but what we assess for purposes of empirical prediction studies is evaluations of performance that may be several steps removed from actual responses. If characteristics of situations exert strong influences on translations of responses into performance, then our prediction of performance using only individual characteristics is extremely poor.

Figure 8 presents a selection model taking these recommendations into consideration. The arrows labeled A and B indicate the mutual influence between individual and situational characteristics. Arrows C and G indicate direct influences of individual and situational characteristics on job responses. Arrows D and E indicate interactions between individual and situational characteristics, and F indicates the effects of these interactions on job responses. Arrow I indicates the effects of job responses on performance; H the effects of situational characteristics on translations of responses into assessed performance. Arrows J, K, L, and M reflect the possibility that responses may change situations and individuals.

This model is not intended as a complete statement of an alternative research paradigm for selection studies. It is presented because we think it represents a reasonable statement of relations among environmental characteristics, individual characteristics, and job performance. Careful examination of the model should lead to selection studies that differ substantially from those nor-

Figure 8. A Situation/Person-Interaction Model of Job Performance and Selection

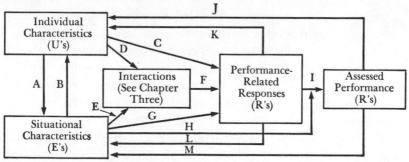

mally encountered. These studies presumably would take into explicit consideration a number of factors now ignored.

Turnover Research

Researchers whose interests are mainly in the effects of individual differences on individual turnover decisions typically assume—or at least conduct research as if they assumed—that the world beyond the walls of the plant or office is there merely to provide organization members a place to live during their time away from their jobs. Researchers whose interests are more macro—sociologists, political scientists, economists—design research as though the environment provided by organizations were a stage on which actors acted out set pieces, pieces whose lines and plots were provided by social values, social movements, and economic trends. As we have seen throughout this book, the strictly individual-differences orientation of psychologists and the macro-level approaches taken by other researchers are both incomplete and possibly misleading. Despite occasional statements about "other" influences on turnover, most investigators continue to design research along strictly disciplinary lines. A notable exception to this trend was provided recently by Mobley (1977), who attempted conceptual synthesis of both sources of variance. March and Simon (1958) also provide a limited cross-disciplinary model that has been honored more by being ignored than by being used.

Economic Factors. The empirical evidence indicates consistent relations between indicators of economic activity, or position in the business cycle, and voluntary turnover. This finding has been documented in the United States and the United Kingdom. Changes in the business cycle reflecting expanding opportunities for employment predict increases in voluntary turnover. Changes in the business cycle reflecting decreased opportunities predict decreases in voluntary turnover. In one of the early studies based on Bureau of Labor Statistics data, Brissenden and Frankel (1922) examined the influence of prevailing business and industrial conditions on voluntary turnover during the period 1910–1918. They found high turnover rates during 1913 and 1917–1918, when the economy was active. Lower turnover rates were observed during

1914–1915, when the economy was less active. Woytinsky (1942) extended this earlier study to cover the period 1910–1940. Voluntary turnover throughout this period was strongly related to economic conditions. Particularly dramatic was the extreme turnover reduction in 1928 and 1929 as economic conditions approached collapse. Palmer (1954) presents evidence that when employment is high, voluntary job changes outnumber involuntary changes. Moreover, voluntary changes made at these times reflect an improvement in workers' economic positions.

After a detailed analysis of business and turnover cycles, Armknecht and Early (1972) note that quit rate in manufacturing is one of the better indicators of business cycles. The curve is smooth and has led the business cycle consistently by fifteen months at its peak and nearly coincided with it at its trough. Armknecht and Early expanded their predictive model to include changes in the new-hire rate in the same and preceding quarters to index availability of alternatives and bank savings rate to index "expectations about the condition of the labor markets." The expanded model accounted for 78 percent of the variance in quit rate. They conclude that changes in quit rate seem to be caused largely by changes in economic factors as well as expectations about future changes.

Gilroy and McIntire (1974) studied relative numbers of job losers, job leavers, and job entrants as a function of industrial production indices. Although there were general increases in the number of unemployed corresponding to decreases in economic activity, the smallest increases in unemployment were found among job leavers. This finding was interpreted as consistent with the notion that workers are reluctant to leave their jobs when the economy weakens.

These relations between economic activity and turnover responses can perhaps best be summarized by noting Eagley's (1965) article. This article reported the correlation between voluntary turnover rates in the United States and economic conditions in the United States for the years 1931–1962. A correlation of .84, explaining about 70 percent of the between-year variance in turnover rates, was obtained. The correlations from the pre- and postwar periods are equivalent.

A careful reading of the accumulated literature relating

economic conditions and turnover, then, suggests that these two variables are strongly related to each other and that this relation has remained consistent from 1910 to the present. We have seen studies analyzing sources of variance in turnover aggregated to the national, industrial, organizational, and departmental levels. In all these studies the results indicate that worsening economic conditions are related to decreases in turnover and that improving economic conditions are related to increases in turnover. The implication throughout this literature is that turnover is *caused* by economic conditions. Behrend (1953, p. 79), among others, explicitly states that "labor turnover as well as absenteeism [is] primarily determined by economic forces." Although causation is assumed by many of these writers, it has not been demonstrated. In fact, such an explanation is only one of a number of viable hypotheses. One hypothesis is that a high rate of economic growth translates into more job opportunities, which, in turn, allow dissatisfied individuals to translate their dissatisfaction into job changes. This and other hypotheses are discussed below.

Organizational/Environmental Factors. Katzell, Barrett, and Parker (1961) analyzed data from 72 comparable but geographically decentralized warehousing divisions. These data were subsequently reanalyzed by Cureton and Katzell (1962). Five variables reflecting unit performance (including its quantity and quality), profitability, and turnover were included. Five additional variables summarizing unit and environmental characteristics (unit size, community size, wage rate, unionization, and proportion of male workers) were also assessed. The results revealed two oblique factors explaining the interrelations among these ten variables. The first factor was associated negatively with division and community size and positively with productivity and profitability. The second was associated negatively with wage rate, unionization, and proportion of male employees and positively with turnover. The oblique angle between the two factors suggests that turnover, although most strongly related to the variables defining the second factor, is also related to division and community size. Divisions whose situational characteristics are in the direction of the small-town culture pattern typically have lower turnover rates.

Kerr, Koppelmeir, and Sullivan (1951) reported data from 892 workers aggregated to the departmental level (twenty-nine departments). These data suggest that departments with high turnover were characterized by having many employees, low rates of unexcused absenteeism, incentive work structure, and little opportunity for conversation among workers.

Evan (1963) examined the effects of being an isolate or a member of a dyad (as opposed to having at least two peers assigned to one's work location) on turnover among science and engineering trainees. Trainees with two or more peers had a turnover rate of 10 percent; those with no peers or only one peer had a turnover rate of about 50 percent.

Ley (1966) presented evidence that supervisor authoritarianism is related to absenteeism and turnover. Ley found that authoritarianism among eighteen plant foremen, as rated by their superiors, accounted for about 50 percent of the variance in turnover rates in work sections.

In overview, results of research relating organizational factors to turnover are sparse and incomplete. Only a few of the many possible organizational characteristics have been related to turnover levels among employees. The data available are hard to integrate. In the typical study, turnover decisions are aggregated to the level of the work group or the department. Organizational subunits occasionally are treated as the units of analysis. Organization or department size appears to be a popular variable to use to predict turnover. Size is also very likely confounded with numerous individual as well as other organizational characteristics, making clear interpretations difficult. Large group or department size appears to predict turnover, although being an isolate or a member of a dyad also predicts turnover at the individual level.

Individual Factors: Job Attitudes. The literature on job attitudes and turnover is reviewed by Porter and Steers (1973) and seems consistent and reasonably well integrated. Job attitudes, usually in the form of job satisfaction, are related to subsequent turnover by individuals. The strength of the relation is such that job satisfaction explains about 10–15 percent of the variance in turnover. Literature appearing since the publication of this review has not significantly changed the overall interpretation. Rather, recent studies have attempted to specify the general conditions in which one could expect the relations between attitudes and turnover to be significant.

Herman (1973), Getman, Goldberg, and Herman (1976), and Smith (1977) discuss the part played by situational constraints on responses in determining observed attitude/behavior relations. Briefly, Herman (1973) presents an argument based on freedom of individual choice as a determiner of attitude/response relations. In situations in which individuals are free to behave as they wish, attitudes indeed predict responses. Smith (1977) tested this hypothesis and found that attendance at work (aggregated to the departmental level) on a day when an unexpected and severe snowstorm made travel very difficult but possible was significantly positively correlated with average departmental satisfaction. The severity of the snowstorm necessitated supervisors excusing any absenteeism. Therefore, Smith argues, attendance was under the control of the individual and was not required by work rules or norms. We cannot expect attitudes to be related to job-withdrawal behaviors universally. In appropriate conditions, however, the relations should be observed.

Background Factors. Standard biographical information blanks or application blanks seem to be major sources of information used in attempts to predict job withdrawal. Results are generally significant, although cross-validation attempts are rare and results frequently appear to be strongly situationally bound and may lack any generalizability.

Trends emerging from this research can be briefly summarized. For many organizations the composite picture of the ideal long-tenure employee is one who is married with children, is older rather than younger, is not college educated, had infrequent job changes in the past, frequently participates in outside activities related to present work activities, was referred by a present employee of the company, and lives close to the place of work. It must be stressed that most of the data providing this profile were obtained from samples of clerical workers and are not terribly exciting. For representative studies see Buel (1964), Kirchner and Dunnette (1957), Kriedt and Gadel (1953), Minor (1958), Mosel and Wade

(1951), and Robinson (1972). Schwab and Oliver (1974) present some arguments suggesting that the usefulness of biographical information blanks is overestimated in the literature.

Implications and Confusions. The literature seems consistent in at least two research areas. First, indicators of economic activity or business cycles are consistently related to turnover. Economic indicators, aggregated by year, account for 70 percent of the variance in voluntary turnover, also aggregated by year, in the United States (1931–1962). Second, we observe consistencies between measures of job attitudes and job-withdrawal behavior. Employees who are satisfied are less likely to leave their jobs than those who are not satisfied. However, the large amount of variance in job withdrawal apparently controlled by economic factors comes as bitter medicine to one identified with the individual-differences branch of psychology. Because of expected unreliability in any response, one might think that explaining 70 percent of the variance in aggregated turnover by aggregated economic measures amounted to explaining all the nonerror variance. The economic explanation does not reflect the entire picture, however, since within any single time period, and therefore with economic conditions held constant, we note interindustry differences in turnover, organizational differences within an industry, and individual differences within organizations, industries, and short time periods. Individual differences in attitudes predicted about 15 percent of the variance in job withdrawal when several relevant individual characteristics (sex, age, marital status, cultural background) as well as organizational factors were held constant (Hulin, 1966b). The 70 percent variance in aggregated turnover data explained by economic conditions very likely is redundant to a certain extent with the variance explained by job attitudes and organizational factors.

March and Simon (1958) propose a model that attempts to reflect contributions of both local-labor-market factors and individual factors to leaving one's job. Turnover is a function of ease of leaving, determined by economic factors such as availability of jobs and individual factors relating to employability, and desirability of leaving, determined by the attractiveness of the current job as assessed by job satisfaction. Economic conditions influence turnover through availability of other jobs, and individual factors influence turnover both through availability of other jobs and through job satisfaction. There is some indirect support for this model. Evidence exists that local economic conditions have a direct effect on job satisfaction (Hulin, 1966a; Kendall, 1963) as well as an inferred effect on perceptions of the ease of leaving a current job. Individual factors of age, sex, race, educational level, job level, and tenure also covary directly with satisfaction (Hulin and Smith, 1964, 1965) and influence the perceived ease of leaving one's current job. Thus, the two explanatory factors used by March and Simon share many antecedents. Disentangling the independent contributions to turnover will be difficult.

Turnover from an Interactionist Viewpoint. Attempts to synthesize research on turnover should look at three factors: effects of the economy (E's), organizational factors (E's), and a hobo factor (U), probably present in different amounts in all of us. Organizational factors (E's) are assumed to affect job withdrawal (R) through their effects on job attitudes. Economic factors are perhaps the most complex. We do not have data to determine whether the economy influences job withdrawal directly by providing more and better jobs for individuals to choose from. The perception of an abundance of other jobs may cause workers to try to upgrade their job status. Alternatively, economic conditions may influence job withdrawal directly by influencing job satisfaction. We also have evidence that job satisfaction influences job withdrawal independently of the influence of economic conditions. The large number of studies summarized by Porter and Steers (1973), each conducted in one location and over a short time period, provide this evidence, since fixing location and time holds economic conditions constant. The indirect explanation of the effects of the economy on job withdrawal argues that external events (economic conditions) are perceived and responded to by workers. These external events are translated into different affective responses and appear to influence job withdrawal, but the direct, or proximal, causes of the withdrawal are individual differences in job attitudes. A third explanation is that economic factors enhance or moderate the relation between job satisfaction and job withdrawal as well as having a direct effect on both variables. During recessions the relation between job satisfaction and job withdrawal is low but still significant and negative. During economic expansion the level of job withdrawal is higher (and satisfaction lower) and the relation between job withdrawal and job satisfaction may be stronger because low base rates are not restricting relations.

The "hobo factor" is taken into account by hypothesizing that even during severe depression, the job-withdrawal rate does not drop to zero, and job satisfaction is still negatively related to job withdrawal. The tendency to migrate from job to job or from city to city may place a floor under the voluntary withdrawal rate. Even in 1932 the voluntary turnover rate was not zero.

Although the literature *can* be integrated, invocations of "faith validity" are necessary, and the resulting explanatory model is shakier than one would wish. Serious problems are apparent when one realizes that the picture painted by research conducted in any one discipline, and hence consonant with the level of aggregation favored in that discipline, not only is incomplete but may prove misleading to both theoreticians and practitioners. If a member of a business organization approached an organizational scientist with a macrolevel, economics background asking for consultation on abnormally high turnover rates in a number of organizational subunits, the advice given would likely be in the language of local labor markets, economic conditions, and business activity. The advice might be simply "Pray for a recession in areas where the subunits are located but not in areas where the products of the subunits are sold." Individual satisfaction and attitudes, supervisory style, or even job design might never be mentioned. The advice would be correct but incomplete: A recession might well reduce abnormally high turnover rates in certain organizational subunits. At the same time, the advice suggests that influences of variables that members of the organization can change are minimal and that organizations are at the mercy of external events over which they have little control. Abnormally high turnover rates in a number of subunits might, rather, be due to internal influences: autocratic managers, poor task design, poor task/person fits among workers, poor communication within the units, or low levels of satisfaction caused by capricious application of pay and promotion policies.

Consider now the advice given by an organizational scientist with a microlevel, psychological background to the same organization member. The advice would likely be to examine a large number of internal variables similar to those outlined in the preceding paragraph. This advice would ignore any possible direct influence of economic conditions on turnover. The economy, if it played any role, would enter only indirectly, by way of its influence on satisfaction.

If taken, these two sets of advice would result essentially in a random distribution of rewards to managers of the organizational subunits. An organization member following advice given by a macrolevel consultant would not consider turnover in an evaluation of subunit managers. He or she would assume that turnover was externally caused and was not an appropriate basis for either year-end bonuses or negative evaluations—even if some managers in areas undergoing substantial economic expansion had been able to keep turnover to a minimum and other managers in depressed areas had had high turnover in spite of low availability of other jobs. An organization member following a psychological consultant's advice would reward managers of subunits with low turnover even though low turnover was caused by a local recession and would negatively evaluate managers of subunits with high turnover. The Panglossian world of insufficient rewards is a fact of life, but we, as organizational scientists, should not compound it by adding randomness to the distribution of the few rewards that are available.

If we recognize the complexities of turnover studies, we will see that we need investigations that allow external environmental conditions, internal organizational characteristics, and individual differences to vary in such a fashion that the effects of each can be assessed independently. Only in this way will we be able to determine the direct and indirect influences of environmental and organizational characteristics on individual behaviors. It might well be that the impressive amount of variance in aggregated turnover decisions is mediated largely through the effects of economic conditions on satisfaction, satisfaction being the proximal cause. We are not arguing that this is the likely causal sequence. We can make *no* argument, because we have no data that will allow us to choose the correct model.

Studies such as those just outlined are neither easy nor inexpensive to conduct. They require a sufficiently large number of organizational units in locations with different economic conditions to allow accurate estimation of the influence of these factors. They require a large enough number of subunits with different organizational characteristics to enable us to estimate organizational effects. They also require sizable numbers of employees in each subunit to enable us to estimate the magnitude of the influences of individual differences within units. In short, we need sizable samples of organizations, not because organizations are our units of analysis but because we must be able to estimate accurately both the within-unit and the between-unit influences on individual decisions. That such studies require much time and money should not lead us to continue to design research we know is incorrect and will lead to misinterpretation. We should look for the wallet where it was dropped, not under the streetlight because we can see better there.

We must reiterate that we are not arguing that past research is of little value. We are arguing that organizational researchers study extremely complex problems that are influenced by variables from a number of levels, as past research has told us very clearly. The necessary next step is to design research based on the information generated from our early, overly simple view of behavior in organizations. We have selected for discussion the two areas of selection and turnover research because there is an extensive literature relevant to both problems, because disciplinary myopia is prevalent in both cases, and because past research should have taught us to approach the study of these problems. We have, apparently, not learned our lessons well.

At the same time, the application of our framework suggests different approaches to the study of old (and unsolved) problems. Empirical data testifying to its benefits are slowly being generated.

CHAPTER 6

Perspectives on Research and Theory Building

This last chapter has two major purposes: to summarize the main points made in the preceding pages and to provide a perspective from which to view research and theory-building efforts. In this latter endeavor, we are not sure what results will be generated by adopting frameworks similar to the one we presented. We are sure, however, that continued emphasis on narrower and narrower views of responses made by individuals in organizations, concentration on individual differences to the exclusion of environmental effects, or concentration on organizational variables to the exclusion of individual differences or societal variables will generate more-precise knowledge about increasingly trivial matters. The long-term result for organizational science will be disastrous.

Review

In Chapter One we provided a rough outline of what is being done and what should be done in organizational science. We noted several important reasons for studying organizations and indicated what organizational researchers and theorists should and should not attempt to explain. Our emphasis was on observing and explaining regularities in the occurrence of events—individual responses, aggregated responses in organizational settings, and even outcomes unique to intact groups and organizations. Only after this step is taken should researchers and theorists focus on irregularities. Part of the problem is determining what events are worth studying, because they rarely come so labeled, and even determining which ones occur with any degree of regularity is difficult.

Researchers and theorists from strikingly different backgrounds actively pursue knowledge about organizations. This diversity results in a special set of problems in that they use in their theories units of analysis ranging from individuals to entire nations. We do not know whether the resulting variables, often labeled identically, represent the same processes or outcomes at different levels of aggregation. A great many of our problems are caused by invoking the same or highly similar explanatory models and theories when we change levels of aggregation without assessing the functional similarity or dissimilarity of these models and theories across levels. Similarly, integration of data bases, languages, models, and theories from different disciplines with their different units of analysis is nearly impossible, given the present scattered state of knowledge and lack of integrating frameworks.

We emphasized that attempts to understand regularities in organizations should focus on developing complex networks of relations among multiple manifestations of multiple constructs. While acknowledging that interpretations of complex networks are flawed and involve biases, filtration of information, and after-the-fact sense-making, we argued that awareness of these facts should not lead to abandoning tough-mindedness in favor of introspection and experiencing as routes to scientific or generalized knowing. Finally, we noted how the structure and approaches of organizational science must differ from those of other social and physical sciences. To be complete, a statement in organizational science must encompass units of analysis from individuals to interacting organizations, forcing us to borrow heavily from work done at many levels of analysis and aggregation.

In the second chapter we presented four distinct, general approaches taken by researchers and theorists to organizational research. These are the research paradigms adopted by human factors specialists, industrial-organizational psychologists, social psychologists, and sociologists. Explicit identification of paradigms underlying studies of organizations is seldom seen but is important, because paradigms determine the nature of theory and the levels of analysis, measurement methods, tasks, groups, and organizational characteristics thought to be important. Our refereed journals are filled with empirical work and theoretical developments to which inappropriate methods, measurement, and analyses follow from researchers' failure to be clear about the paradigms from which they operate and from their failure to take broader views of concepts and problems.

Different approaches to the study of communication were used to illustrate the impact of paradigms on our research on organizational issues. Although designed to reflect factors relevant to particular organizational activities studied, paradigms act as perceptual filters determining how students of organizations view the processes they study. Beyond simply limiting how we perceive organizational processes, paradigms reinforce our limited perspectives and make it hard to integrate theory and research from one discipline to another.

The four paradigms discussed in Chapter Two do not exhaust those used in all of organizational science. Researchers from other disciplines, including political science and economics, make contributions to the study of organizations. We excluded these disciplines because their generally macro levels of analysis make it questionable that their results can be integrated with those from disciplines that recognize that, ultimately, individuals respond in organizations and provide us with what should be recognized as our basic data. Even organizational structures and interdependencies are results of things people do.

We began Chapter Three by delineating a few terms for which there is good agreement about meanings among organizational researchers and theorists. These terms were defined and were used to develop a parsimonious but static blueprint, or framework, to guide research efforts. The framework was then expanded to include time as a component. The inclusion of time moved us from a static to a dynamic view of organizations, in which focus on the structural units of analysis is supplemented by considerations of process. An example was offered of research that could be designed using this strategy. In this example we showed how responses observed at one point in time might influence characteristics of the situation at a later time. We also addressed the question of whether organizational research and theory would benefit from the considerations we had raised. Finally, in Chapter Three we noted that some responses are unique to individuals, some to groups, and some to entire organizations. Responses attached to units ranging from individuals to organizations in size suggest the use of an integrated research approach rather than a continued emphasis on a misleading micro/macro split within this field of research.

The discussion of problems of aggregation in Chapter Four provides the most abstract treatment of research problems we take up in this book. It is also the least satisfying to us, because, although we present numerous problems, we provide few solutions. This is especially disquieting because we are convinced that aggregation problems are potentially the most serious problems faced by organizational researchers. At this time we can only say that potential impacts of aggregation on research and theory must be addressed before solutions can be developed. Theories of composition are needed to augment the content and process theories currently available in organizational science.

We noted the following difficulties in the use of different kinds of aggregation: *Theories* frequently fail to specify units of analysis (individual, group, or organization) or types of constructs (global or aggregate). *Samples* are often selected without reference to the units of theory to which they are supposedly relevant; little thought is given to sample boundaries appropriate to the questions posed by the research. *Time* is usually forgotten altogether in both research and theory, with the result that inferences based on inappropriate time intervals may be meaningless. Longitudinal studies focusing on processes rather than outcomes are completely dependent on correct selection of observation intervals. *Measurement* fails to take into account explicitly that assessed variables are compositions or results of events that happen and variables that interact and that the events and variables are often reciprocally causal. Explicit attention has not been paid to grouping procedures in *data analyses,* resulting in a high probability of meaningless results. Specification errors are frequent in *interpretation* of results, leading, of course, to highly equivocal interpretations.

We also mentioned assignment of group-level scores to individuals and some problems that result from this practice and from disaggregation. Assignment of group-level scores to individuals, we believe, does not impede research progress so seriously as aggregation does—mainly because a macrolevel score can be assigned to a more micro-level unit, as a reflection of the environment within which the unit functions, without serious interpretational problems. Some aggregation problems can be addressed and solutions provided, such as the development of theories into which time enters explicitly. Simply sensitizing ourselves to aggregation issues should aid us in articulating potential sources of error in research and theory construction. A plea to keep our wits about us and remember at all times what we are trying to accomplish by means of our research efforts and theory development may suffice to prevent gross misinterpretations from occurring while solutions to aggregation problems are being sought.

Chapter Five shows what might occur if one tried to integrate past research or design new research on selection and turnover problems using the framework provided in Chapter Three. Turnover was chosen because it has been studied by researchers from a number of disciplines. Even though it has, there has been little integration of findings. Selection has typically been investigated only by researchers with individual-differences approaches. Study of selection by members of a single discipline, psychology, has resulted in wholesale ignoring of potential influences of relevant macro-level variables. At the same time, the research frameworks used to design selection research come from a static, trait-oriented theoretical tradition that assumes that changes in individuals over time are little more than random fluctuations of little consequence. The depressing state of knowledge combined with lack of progress in the selection area over the past half century should lead us to serious questioning of all assumptions implicit in our various paradigms. Chapter Five shows that selection research generated from a dynamic, person/situation-interactionist framework would be substantially different from what exists and would contain possibilities for examining the validity of the many assumptions we make.

Turnover research is decidedly different. In this area no one discipline has dominated. We reviewed studies ranging from macro to micro, from turnover aggregated to the level of an entire nation during a year to individual decisions to leave a particular organization during a specified time interval. Although heterogeneity of disciplinary approaches is positive, it has been accompanied by few serious attempts to bridge gaps between disciplines, to integrate different and apparently contradictory findings, or to design unifying studies integrating the strengths of different approaches. For both turnover and selection research, we attempted to point out inconsistencies and problems resulting from failure to treat individual behavior with the complexity it deserves. Research designed within a framework that explicitly recognizes the influence of both individual and environmental variables would provide an opportunity to generate more-comprehensive models of turnover and to test these broader models.

Chapter Five was not an exercise in criticizing past research efforts. Clearly, we have built on past findings in attempts to summarize and integrate what we know about selection and turnover. We intended to suggest that the accumulated findings indicate that past research designs were too narrow and that it is time to move ahead with broader research approaches to these and other persistent organizational problems.

Perspective on Research and Theory

Public Policy and Research Populations. One motive for writing this book is our desire to see innovation in our field. We have a second motive. It is important that organizational researchers maintain perspective on what they and others do with the data they generate. Much of what we read is regarded as basic research by investigators who are properly concerned about the internal validity of their studies. Such concern is important. Most of us, however, seem startlingly unconcerned with the external validity of our conclusions and populations to which we may safely generalize. Thus, we neither provide assessments of important environmental characteristics operating in our studies nor provide adequate statements about boundaries beyond which our conclusions probably do not hold.

An example of such use of data is provided by the report *Work in America* (HEW Task Force, 1973), prepared by a social anthropologist. One theme in this report is that increased job satisfaction is followed by increased productivity—a highly questionable interpretation of the literature on job satisfaction and performance. Quite aside from the serious errors of reporting and summarizing data accurately and drawing valid conclusions in the book, this theme is a clear example of the use of social science data by a federal agency to support public-policy decisions and proposed legislation. These and other data on job satisfaction and quality of working life in the United States have been used to support the Quality of Work program under the Federal Price Commission, the National Center for Productivity and Quality of Working Life, and a bill sponsored by Representative Stanley Ludine (D., N.J.) called the Human Resources Development Act. This bill would have provided $25 million for fiscal year 1978 for "innovative" projects designed to upgrade job skills, redesign jobs, and establish joint union/management committees to increase job satisfaction and decrease counterproductive behavior.

Another example of the use of organizational science data to influence public policy is found in legislation revising some provisions of the National Labor Relations Act (NLRA). The United States Senate report on this bill leans heavily on a single study—Getman, Goldberg, and Herman (1976). This project studied thirty-one union certification elections conducted in the Midwest. The findings and conclusions, although hardly surprising to a social scientist, raised serious questions about the assumptions made by National Labor Relations Board (NLRB) members in overturning certification elections.

Getman, Goldberg, and Herman found, for example, that workers' attitudes about unions and their companies before the thirty-day campaign were extremely accurate predictors of how they would vote in certification elections (twenty-nine of the thirty-one outcomes could have been predicted given a knowledge of these precampaign attitudes), that most workers were unable to recall the content of union or company campaigns, and that unfair labor practices had little effect on election outcomes. Because the NLRB overturns hundreds of elections every year at a substantial cost, revisions of provisions of the NLRA are important. They are also important to organized labor because liberalizing what parties to elections can say and do in an election campaign *may* affect unionization drives.

The reliance by the Senate subcommittee on the empirical study by Getman, Goldberg, and Herman is preferred to reliance on NLRB members' poorly informed opinions about how communication influences behavior. However, such reliance may exceed what is justified by the external validity of the conclusions. That all thirty-one elections occurred in the Midwest raises problems of environmental influences on generalizations. Whether similar results would have been obtained in more militantly pro- or anti-union regions of the United States is unknown. Getman, Goldberg, and Herman expressly discuss these limitations.

None of us is naive enough to believe that current interest in quality of working life in the United States came about because of the more than 5,000 published studies of job satisfaction. Similarly, the existence of Getman, Goldberg, and Herman's data is not solely to blame for the current deliberations over the NLRA. Nevertheless, data obtained by organizational researchers are being used to influence social policy in the United States in ways that may never have been intended by the researchers who generated the data.

Because of the way organizational scientists currently do their work, their studies are restricted to about 9 percent of the organizations in the United States, those with fifty or more employees. We equate *organization* with *establishment,* defined by the Bureau of the Census as "a business or industrial unit at a single physical location which produces or distributes goods or performs services" (U.S. Bureau of Census, 1972, p. 164). The minimum number of employees is usually set (more or less arbitrarily) at fifty because of increasing trends in organizational science toward use of multivariate designs demanding large samples. Although the 9 percent of organizations we can study employ the majority of the workers in the United States, our generalizations are normally made to individuals working in organizations, without regard for the characteristics of the organizations. If our data are gathered from a size-biased sample limited to 9 percent of the organizations in the United States, generalizations outside this restricted population may be unwarranted.

The restriction on whom we can study in what organizations is further complicated by the realization that the organizations we are *allowed* to study very likely represent a badly biased sample from among the already biased 9 percent we are *capable* of studying. We do not know whether the organizations into which we gain entree are those with problems their managers are most willing to accept help to solve or whether they are the organizations with the fewest problems, in which managers can afford to allow their employees to spend an hour or more complying with requests from researchers. We can easily conjure up reasons managers in expanding, profitable firms or managers in marginal firms with severe problems might decide to welcome us or deny us entry.

The solution to the problem of degrees of freedom and sample size is not to circumvent problems of organizational size by obtaining national probability samples combining individuals from large numbers of organizations into one undifferentiated sample to study response consistencies. If one wishes to learn about consistencies in processes and responses that are free of situational or temporal influence, such samples are appropriate. Such research methods remove individuals from their social and organizational contexts and destroy the integrity of the person/organization unit, which, we believe, is a necessary part of studying responses in organizations. Combining individuals from many organizations to produce large samples indeed solves the problem of degrees of freedom. Unfortunately, we buy degrees of freedom at the cost of ability to estimate anything but total effects of independent variables: we are unable to estimate either between- or within-organization effects. Because we should be concerned with the generalizability of our within-organization effects, such sampling procedures seem inappropriate.

Scientific and Social Values of Organizational Scientists. A problem of potentially equal impact on our data base is related to the values of organizational scientists, organization managers, and decision makers in research-funding agencies. Although most of us pretend that we are apolitical in our research and that our values have little to do with what or whom we study, a little thought suggests otherwise. Our research is by no means value-free. We make certain assumptions about the role of organizations in society. We generally assume that organizations are a legitimate source of influence over our everyday lives. For example, we do little research to support or even address the notion that organizations with assets greater than $1 million ought to be abolished. The predominance in our research of dependent variables related to or reflecting productivity and efficiency suggests acceptance of a managerial perspective. As Dachler and Wilpert (1978, p. 9) observe in research on participation, "Research in the productivity and efficiency tradition limits participatory arrangements in scope and intensity, and characteristically leaves them under complete control of management, so that there is no intended challenge to the basic power prerogative of business leaders."

To a large extent, we accept the prerogatives of management to influence employees, to mold them, or to select them to create work forces having certain characteristics. Further, we provide such techniques as testing, management by objectives, and job design to facilitate manipulations of employees. Unlike experimentation that requires informed consent by participants, however, programs on attitude change and job design do not necessarily involve participant approval when conducted within an organization. Concern with the values reflected in organizational research is not new; it is expressed by Baritz (1960) in his history of social science in industry, as well as by others. However, concern about assumptions we make as organizational scientists is perhaps more salient now than ever before as social science increases its influence on public policy.

Our values and assumptions, in the form of the paradigms discussed in Chapter Two, may shape not only the content but the methods of our research. To a large extent, the study of organizations has long followed what Szent-Gyorgi (1972) termed an Apollonian mode. Here science tends to develop along well-established lines toward greater precision. The paradigms of human factors specialists, psychologists, and sociologists are examples of such a model. The Apollonian model contrasts with the Dionysian model, a problem-solving approach, more apt to open new lines of research conforming to no existing paradigm.

Differences between Szent-Gyorgi's Apollonian and Dionysian models are not merely academic. The progress of organizational science depends largely on the support our research attracts. Present methods of distributing support in the form of grants give preference to the Apollonian researcher. According to Szent-Gyorgi, "Applying for a grant begins with writing a project. The Apollonian clearly sees the future lines of his research and has no difficulty writing a clear project. Not so the Dionysian, who knows only the direction in which he wants to go out into the unknown; he has no idea what he is going to find there and how he is going to find it" (p. 966).

The Apollonian model of building on a well-established body of knowledge (as is done, for example, in research on job attitudes and perception of job characteristics) permeates organizational science. Existing paradigms and the Apollonian model make the study of newly established or nontraditional organizations difficult (for example, through demands for large sample sizes in single-organization studies). Our Apollonian model may be based not only on grantsmanship and our knowledge of what is likely to be funded (always a concern to some extent) but also on an implicit assumption about what constitutes an organization. The Dionysian, who opens new avenues of research, is less constrained by the present state of the art.

We are faced with a dilemma. While organizational science data are used to generate and justify public policies affecting us as citizens, we are becoming increasingly aware as scientists of the biased data sources at our disposal. Restricting applications of policy to those organizations to which generalizations are most reasonable might be viewed by courts as a violation of the equal protection guaranteed us by the Fourteenth Amendment to the Constitution. Suggesting to policy makers that they should not rely on organizational data for information would be professional suicide, since we must rely on external support for conducting research whose magnitude will have any value.

The dilemma is further confounded when we make explicit the three audiences to our research and theory-building efforts. For most of us, peers and colleagues are an important part of this constituency. Managers in organizations who adopt or reject our recommendations are another important segment to those of us hoping to make an impact on organizational practice through our research. Finally, we have to respond to the needs of funding agencies, needs brought about by *their* two masters—other organizational scientists and members of Congress.

We argue nevertheless for a shift in emphasis from tightly constrained Apollonian research models to less restricted Dionysian models. By using Dionysian models, organizational scientists are building on what we have learned by past research efforts. We are also reacting to the even larger number of things organizational scientists have *not* learned from past research. A break with past traditions and paradigms seems necessary if organizational scientists are to continue to have any influence on either organizational practice or public policy. Basic research, almost by definition, implies ventures from the known into the unknown. To the extent that we allow ourselves to become too enmeshed in the known, safe, and secure research areas, perhaps because of a fear that our hypotheses will not be verified or we will not be funded, ventures into nontraditional, unknown, and unpopular areas will not be made.

Determining External Validities. We are faced with unresolved issues. One need is to develop a method that helps us place limits on the external validity of our findings and allows statements about generalizing them to organizations not studied. Such a procedure requires specifications of characteristics of organizations and their work forces that are relevant for limiting generalizations. Available taxonomies on organizations provide little guidance and are of extremely limited usefulness for determining limits of external validity. Basically, taxonomies provide sets of dimensions or characteristics to apply in locating organizations in different cells of taxonomic tables. Our argument is that taxonomies, while achieving the stated goal, tell us very little about the behavior of individuals in organizations or similarities of behavior patterns across people in different organizations. Taxonomies consisting entirely of characteristics of organizations without reference either to individual members of them or to the extent to which these characteristics influence individual responses seem of limited value.

Perhaps it is in this endeavor that a tightly constrained Apollonian research model can make important contributions toward more integrative research. Resemblances among mathematical representations of organizations can be computed. (*Resemblance* is here being used in the strict mathematical sense of a measure of generalized distance.) As long as the elements entering the vectors representing different organizations are characteristics of those organizations and their work forces shown previously to be related to individual or aggregated responses, resemblances between pairs of organizations should reflect the degree to which findings would replicate across the same pairs. This procedure will enable a person following a Dionysian research model to venture into less-well-known worlds—worlds of volunteer organizations, not-for-profit organizations, organizations staffed differently than those we usually study, and so on—the ventures into the unknown being launched from the known and guided by mathematical resemblances. That is, resemblances can be calculated between organizations that have been studied exhaustively and organizations that might be legitimate targets of inquiry for those of us following less-traveled roads. If research indicates that we can expect replication of results between studied organizations that resemble each other, and if we can compute degrees of resemblance, then our findings and our approaches could be more confidently applied to new populations of organizations not previously studied. Policy decisions affecting members of organizations studied and not studied could be generally applied with similar confidence.

The procedure outlined briefly above will very likely provide a partial solution to our need to place limits on generalizations and to provide entree into new domains of organizations. The exploration of new research is necessary if we are to avoid intradisciplinary senescence. A first step toward a new approach to organizational research comes with questioning past methods. This book is intended as such a first step. We are concerned with the use of rigorous methods of reseach, but we are less concerned with perfecting any given method than with the substance of research in organizational science. Because of this concern for substance, the Dionysian approach offers an intriguing supplement to existing research models.

Perhaps the Dionysian is one who believes that discovery awaits off the beaten path of our paradigms because the valuable finds along the well-traveled courses may have been scooped up long ago. Since discovery means a departure from existing knowledge, perhaps it is necessary to expand our knowledge of organizations and responses of individuals within them, to move away from our paradigms to less-traveled roads that facilitate classification, observation, and description rather than precise assessments and model building. We need to move away from the paradigms of human factors, psychology, and sociology. We need to establish new paradigms designed specifically for organizational science.

Concluding Remarks

"*Points*, incidentally, is the great common word of academics. . . . [An academic] takes points, follows them, notes them, is struck by them, makes them. Points can be interesting, provocative, simple, borrowed, old-fashioned, novel. . . . One also points to things, sections of academic papers, stages in an argument. . . . But I have heard (and treasure) 'if I may point again to my point'" (Aitken, 1976, p. 28). We have but one "point" to stress in our concluding remarks.

The long, arduous, sometimes onerous activities involved in the development of a discipline (scientific or otherwise), in a single research program, or in any other line of investigation are too often overlooked. The various activities typical of segments in these developments are too often ignored. One should not expect that the expenditure of one's time and energy will necessarily result in fame, fortune, and a singularly important contribution to organizational science. More often than not, it does not.

The histories of the natural sciences show that in its embryonic stages, each of our modern disciplines was characterized by violent polemics rather than reasoned opinion. The reader who does not think organizational research is rife with controversy (perhaps because of the bland way controversies are dealt with in journal articles and books) need only think back to the last faculty meeting he or she attended or heard about concerned with hiring, firing, or promoting an "organizational scholar." Alternatively, listening in on the deliberations of review panels in agencies that dispense research grants can be equally enlightening. Squabbles abound, and it often seems that no three persons interested in organizational research can agree on the competence of a fourth, the content of research that should be encouraged, or the way it should be done. As in each of the older disciplines, however, each new generation tends to see how the values and prejudices of predecessors proved to be stumbling blocks to progress. Simply seeing this is progress. But along with increased visual acuity comes the raising of standards for impartiality.

Science is anything but simple. If we are willing to agree that those of us interested in organizational research will one day be regarded as scientists (whether organizational research is a science constitutes one current controversy), we need only look at other sciences in order to become less concerned about the length of the trek we are taking. Conant (1951, pp. 29–30) remarks on the slowness of science:

> Why did it take so long a period of fumbling before scientists were clear on some very familiar matters? Newton's famous work was complete by the close of the seventeenth century. The cultured gentlemen of France and England in the first decades of the eighteenth century talked in terms of a solar system almost identical with that taught in school today. The laws of motion and their application to mechanics were widely understood. Yet it was not until the 1770s that the common phenomenon of combustion was formulated in terms of comparable clarity; it was not until much later that the concept of heat as "a mode of motion"

was accepted. Spontaneous generation of life, you will recall, was an open question as late as the 1870s. Seventy-five
years ago the professor of natural philosophy at Harvard
told his classes that "people now accept the undulatory
theory of light because all those who formerly accepted the
corpuscular theory are dead." The implied prophecy in this
bit of skepticism turned out to be not far from the mark.
Only within the lifetime of many of us has it been possible to
develop concepts which take care of relatively simple facts
concerning the emission and absorption of radiant energy.
Darwin convinced himself and later the scientific world and
later still the educated public of the correctness of the general idea of evolution because of a theory as to the
mechanism by which evolution might have occurred. Today,
the basic idea of the evolutionary development of higher
plants and animals stands without question, but Darwin's
mechanism has been so greatly questioned as to have been
almost overthrown. And we are no nearer a solution of the
problem of how life originated on this planet than we were
in Darwin's day.

The stumbling way to which even the ablest of the
early scientists had to fight through thickets of erroneous
observations, misleading generalizations, inadequate for-
mulations, and unconscious prejudice is the story which
seems to me needs telling.

The three-hundred-year lag between the developments of
seventeenth century physics that were basic to putting men on the
moon in the twentieth century should not be a cause for pessimism.
Rather, it should be an encouragement about what we are ac-
complishing. That these basic developments, stemming from pure
research, were contributory at all is the important fact to keep in
mind. Most of the participants in all phases of this accomplishment
had a good time exploring ideas, fumbling along toward the goal of
a moon landing. But the small steps and the backward steps had to
be expected and accepted along with the "giant leap."

Even within single research programs, the plodding behavior of the participants is apparent and should be sympathized
with, if not entered into. The solution of the structure of DNA, the
fundamental genetic material, is one of the most exciting scientific
activities of the twentieth century (and one that brought fame and
fortune to some of its participants). The nature of the excitement

as well as the disappointments involved in various stages of this research are vividly recorded by Watson (1968): "My first X-ray pictures revealed, not unexpectedly, much less detail than was found in the published pictures. Over a month was required before I could get even halfway presentable pictures" (p. 78). "My doo dling of the bases on paper at first got nowhere. . . . Not until the middle of the next week . . . did a nontrivial idea emerge" (p. 116) "My scheme was torn to shreds by the following noon. Against me was the awkward chemical fact that I had chosen the wrong tautomeric forms of guanine and thymine" (p. 120).

Simple blocks along our pathways to understanding provide one problem, wrong turns another. In the fall of 1975, Nobel laureate Owen Chamberlain informally discussed his research in nuclear physics with a group of Ph.D. students in a business school. His remarks about the number of dead ends, blind alleys, and wrong turns that one takes in research struck particularly responsive chords in students trying to learn "the science of muddling through." Sometimes all one can do is muddle through. Chamberlain noted that an interesting thing about scientific research is that one can modify the experiment while it is in process and that previously collected data may still be usable.

The time-consuming plodding combined with the excitement of discovery, the characteristics we are talking about here, are as true of other areas requiring investigation as they are of science. We are probably all a little saddened when we realize that a job analysis of the activities involved in spying would not produce a description we would associate with James Bond. Spying is the often tedious business of tracing down bits and pieces of information, checking and cross-checking them. Probably few spies are as lucky as Bond in where they find their information (as regards both geography and individuals), the high-technology mechanisms they can use in their chase, or even the necessity of and luck involved in getting out alive with a solution.

Returning to reality, there are any number of other investigative activities having the same characteristics. Think of the number of times, if you will, that Bernstein and Woodward (1974) almost gave up in their Watergate investigation, the number of times they were stopped cold in their activities, and the number of wrong leads followed to the inevitable dead end. Analogous stories of accomplishments, failures, and perseverance among most scientists are not nearly so widely or well known.

Most of us will not have the "press" of the Watsons, the Chamberlains, or the Bernsteins and Woodwards. But, then, most of us will not be exposed to the criticisms that these people receive. Although our goals may be more modest than those of Chamberlain, Watson, and others, we all have great potential for contributing to organizational research, understanding this area of scientific inquiry, and taking from it findings applicable to our own organizational worlds.

We hope that in this book we have added something to your understanding and perhaps to the current controversies over how one should think about organizational research. We welcome all commentary. Of course, in the spirit of the unenlightened academician, we already have a few replies (Aitken, 1976, p. 28):

> "I'm glad you raised that point." (*How in hell's name did I miss that?*)
>
> "We may not, after all, be much in disagreement." (*You're probably right, I'll scrap this section when I (re)write it.*)

References

****

Adams, J. A. *Experimental Studies of Human Vigilance.* Technical Report ESD–TDR–63–620. Hanscom Field, Mass.: Electronic Systems Division, 1963.

Aitken, D. "A Helpful Guide to Scholarly Jargon." *San Francisco Examiner-Chronicle,* January 25, 1976.

Allen, T., and Cohen, S. "Information Flow in R & D Laboratories." *Administrative Science Quarterly,* 1969, *4,* 14–20.

Allison, G. *Essence of Decision.* Boston: Little, Brown, 1971.

Alvares, K. M., and Hulin, C. L. "Two Explanations of Temporal Changes in Ability-Skill Relationships: A Literature Review and Theoretical Analysis." *Human Factors,* 1972, *14,* 295–308.

Alvares, K. M., and Hulin, C. L. "An Experimental Evaluation of a Temporal Decay in the Prediction of Performance." *Organizational Behavior and Human Performance,* 1973, *9* (1), 169–185.

Armknecht, P. A., and Early, J. F. "Quits in Manufacturing: A Study of Their Causes." *Monthly Labor Review,* 1972, *11,* 31–37.

Azumi, K., and Hage, J. *Organizational Systems.* Lexington, Mass.: Heath, 1972.

Baritz, L. *The Servants of Power*. New York: Wiley, 1960.

Barton, A. H. "Bringing Society Back in: Survey Research and Macro-Methodology." *American Behavioral Scientist*, 1968, *1*, 1–9.

Bavelas, A. "Communication Patterns in Task-Oriented Groups." *Acoustical Society of America Journal*, 1950, *22*, 727–730.

Behrend, H. "Absence of Labor Turnover in a Changing Economic Climate." *Journal of Occupational Psychology*, 1953, *27*, 69–79.

Bell, G. D. "Determinants of Span of Control." *American Journal of Sociology*, 1967, *73*, 100–109.

Bernstein, C., and Woodward, B. *All the President's Men*. New York: Simon & Schuster, 1974.

Berrien, K. E. "A General Systems Approach to Organizations." In M. D. Dunnette (Ed.) *Handbook of Industrial and Organizational Psychology*. Chicago: Rand McNally, 1976.

Bidwell, C. E., and Kasarda, J. D. "School District Organization and Student Achievement." *American Sociological Review*, 1975, *40*, 55–70.

Bidwell, C. E., and Kasarda, J. D. "Reply to Hannan, Freeman, and Meyer, and Alexander and Griffin." *American Sociological Review*, 1976, *41*, 152–160.

Blalock, H. M. *Causal Inferences in Nonexperimental Research*. Chapel Hill: University of North Carolina Press, 1964.

Blau, P. M., and Schoenherr, R. A. *The Structure of Organizations*. New York: Basic Books, 1971.

Brissenden, P. F., and Frankel, E. *Labor Turnover in Industry*. New York: Macmillan, 1922.

Buckley, W. *Modern Systems Research for the Behavioral Scientist*. Chicago: Aldine, 1968.

Buel, W. "Voluntary Female Clerical Turnover: Concurrent and Predictive Validity of Weighted Application Blank." *Journal of Applied Psychology*, 1964, *48*, 180–182.

Campbell, D. T. "Blind Variation and Selection Retention in Creative Thought as in Other Knowledge Processes." *Psychological Review*, 1960, *67* (6), 380–400.

Campbell, D. T. "Qualitative Knowing in Action Research." Kurt Lewin Award Address presented at joint meeting of Society for the Psychological Study of Social Issues and the American Psychological Association, New Orleans, September 1974.

Chapanis, A. *Man Machine Engineering.* Belmont, Calif.: Wadsworth, 1965.

Cherrington, D. L., Reitz, H. J., and Scott, W. E. "Effects of Reward and Contingent Reinforcements on Satisfactions and Task Performance." *Journal of Applied Psychology,* 1971, *55,* 531–536.

Child, J. "Organization Structure and Strategies of Control: A Replication of the Aston Study." *Administrative Science Quarterly,* 1972, *17,* 163–177.

Child, J. "Strategies of Control and Organizational Behavior." *Administrative Science Quarterly,* 1973, *18,* 1–17.

Coleman, J. S., and others. *Equality of Educational Opportunity.* Report of the Office of Education, U.S. Department of Health, Education, and Welfare. Washington, D.C.: U.S. Government Printing Office, 1966.

Compact Edition of the Oxford English Dictionary. 2 vols. London: Oxford University Press, 1971.

Conant, J. D. *On Understanding Science.* New York: Mentor, 1951.

Cook, T. D., and Campbell, D. T. "The Design and Conduct of Quasi-Experimental and True Experiments in Field Settings." In M. D. Dunnette (Ed.) *Handbook of Industrial and Organizational Psychology.* Chicago: Rand McNally, 1976.

Cortlett, E. N. "Human Factors in the Design of Manufacturing Systems." *Human Factors,* 1973, *15,* 105–110.

Cronbach, L. J., and Meehl, P. F. "Construct Validity in Psychological Tests." *Psychological Bulletin,* 1955, *52,* 281–302.

Cronbach, L. J. *Research on Classrooms and Schools: Formulation of Questions, Design, and Analysis.* Stanford, Calif.: Stanford Evaluation Consortium, 1976.

Cureton, E., and Katzell, R. "A Further Analysis of the Relations Among Job Performance and Situational Variables." *Journal of Applied Psychology,* 1962, *46,* 230.

Dachler, H. P., and Wilpert, B. "Conceptual Dimensions and Boundaries of Participation in Organizations: A Critical Evaluation." *Administrative Science Quarterly,* 1978, *23,* 1–40.

Davis, J. A. *Great Books and Small Groups.* New York: Free Press, 1961.

Drexler, J. A. "Organizational Climate: Its Homogeneity with Organizations." *Journal of Applied Psychology,* 1977, *62,* 38–42.

Dunham, R. B. "Ability-Skill Relationships: An Empirical Explanation of Change over Time." *Organizational Behavior and Human Performance,* 1974, *3* (12), 372–382.

Dunnette, M. D. *Personal Selection and Placement.* Monterey, Calif.: Brooks/Cole, 1966.

Durkheim, E. *The Rules of Sociological Method.* New York: Free Press, 1950.

Durkheim, E. *Suicide, a Study in Sociology.* New York: Free Press, 1951.

Eagley, R. V. "Market Power as an Intervening Mechanism in Phillips Curve Analysis." *Economics,* 1965, *32,* 48–64.

Ekehammar, B. "Interaction in Personality from a Historical Perspective." *Psychological Bulletin,* 1974, *81,* 1026–1048.

Endler, N. S. "The Case for Person-Situation Interactions." *Canadian Psychological Review,* 1975, *16,* 12–21.

Evan, W. M. "Peer Group Interaction and Organizational Socialization: A Study of Employee Turnover." *American Sociological Review,* 1963, *28,* 436–440.

Feldman, J. "Considerations in the Use of Causal-Correlational Techniques in Applied Psychology." *Journal of Applied Psychology,* 1975, *60,* 663–670.

Fiedler, F. E., Chemers, M. M., and Mahar, L. *Improving Leadership Effectiveness.* New York: Wiley, 1976.

Finkle, R. B. "Managerial Assessment Centers." In M. D. Dunnette (Ed.), *Handbook of Industrial and Organizational Psychology.* Chicago: Rand McNally, 1976.

Fiske, D. W. *Strategies for Personality Research: The Observation Versus Interpretation of Behaviors.* San Francisco: Jossey-Bass, 1978.

Forehand, G. A., and Gilmer, B. V. "Environmental Variation in Studies of Organizational Behavior." *Psychological Bulletin,* 1964, *62,* 361–382.

Friedlander, F., and Margulies, N. "Multiple Impacts of Organizational Climate and Individual Value Systems upon Job Satisfaction." *Personnel Psychology,* 1969, *22,* 171–183.

Galtung, J. *Theory and Methods of Social Research.* New York: Columbia University Press, 1967.

Gergen, K. J. "Social Psychology as History." *Journal of Personality and Social Psychology,* 1973, *26,* 309–320.

Getman, J. G., Goldberg, S. B., and Herman, J. B. *Union Representation Elections: Law and Reality.* New York: Russell Sage Foundation, 1976.

Ghiselli, E. E. *The Validity of Occupational Aptitude Tests.* New York: Wiley, 1966.

Gilroy, C. L., and McIntire, R. J. "Job Losers, Leavers, and Entrants: A Cyclical Analysis." *Monthly Labor Review,* 1974, *97* (11), 35–39.

Graen, G. "Role-Making Processes Within Complex Organizations." In M. D. Dunnette (Ed.), *Handbook of Industrial and Organizational Psychology.* Chicago: Rand McNally, 1976.

Griggs v. *Duke Power Company.* 401 U.S. 424 (1971).

Guion, R. M. "A Note on Organizational Climate." *Organizational Behavior and Human Performance,* 1973, *9,* 120–125.

Hackman, J. R. "Group Influences on Organizations." In M. D. Dunnette (Ed.), *Industrial and Organizational Psychology.* Chicago: Rand McNally, 1976.

Hackman, J. R., and Oldham, G. R. "Development of the Job Diagnostic Survey." *Journal of Applied Psychology,* 1975, *60,* 159–170.

Hage, J., and Aiken, M. "Routine Technology, Social Structure, and Organizational Goals." *Administrative Science Quarterly,* 1969, *14,* 366–376.

Hammond, J. H. "Two Sources of Error in Ecological Correlations." *American Sociological Review,* 1973, *38,* 764–777.

Hannan, M. T. *Aggregation and Disaggregation in Sociology.* Lexington, Mass.: Heath, 1971a.

Hannan, M. T. "Problems of Aggregation." In H. M. Blalock (Ed.), *Causal Models in the Social Sciences.* Chicago: Aldine, 1971b.

Hannan, M. T., and Freeman, J. H. "The Population Ecology of Organizations." *American Journal of Sociology,* 1976, *82,* 929–964.

Hannan, M. T., Freeman, J. H., and Meyer, J. W. "Specification of Models for Organizational Effectiveness (Comment on Bidwell and Kasarda, ASR February, 1975)." *American Sociological Review,* 1976, *41,* 136–143.

Hedrick, T. E., Boruch, R. F., and Ross, J. "Policy and Regulation for Ensuring the Availability of Evaluative Data." *Policy Sciences,* in press.

Herman, J. B. "Are Situational Contingencies Limiting Job Attitude-Job Performance Relationships?" *Organizational Behavior and Human Performance*, 1973, *10*, 208–224.

HEW Task Force. *Work in America*. Cambridge, Mass.: M.I.T. Press, 1973.

Hickson, D. J., Pugh, D. S., and Pheysey, D. C. "Operations Technology and Organizational Structure: An Empirical Reappraisal." *Administrative Science Quarterly*, 1969, *14*, 378–397.

House, R. J., and Mitchell, T. R. "Path-Goal Theory of Leadership." *Contemporary Business*, 1974, *3*, 81–97.

Hulin, C. L. "Effects of Community Characteristics on Measures of Job Satisfaction." *Journal of Applied Psychology*, 1966a, *50*, 185–192.

Hulin, C. L. "Job Satisfaction and Turnover in a Female Clerical Population." *Journal of Applied Psychology*, 1966b, *50*, 280–285.

Hulin, C. L., and Smith, P. C. "Sex Differences in Job Satisfaction." *Journal of Applied Psychology*, 1964, *48*, 88–92.

Hulin, C. L., and Smith, P. C. "A Linear Model of Job Satisfaction." *Journal of Applied Psychology*, 1965, *49*, 209–216.

Hull, C. L. *Aptitude Testing*. Chicago: World Book, 1928.

Humphreys, L. G. "The Organization of Human Abilities." *American Psychologist*, 1962, *17*, 475–483.

Humphreys, L. G. "The Fleeting Nature of the Prediction of College Academic Success." *Journal of Educational Psychology*, 1968, *59* (5), 375–380.

Hunt, D. P., Howell, W. C., and Roscoe, S. N. "Educational Programs for Engineering Psychologists." *Human Factors*, 1972, *14*, 77–78.

James, L. R., and others. *Psychological Climate: Implications from Cognitive Social Learning Theory and Interactional Psychology*. Fort Worth: Institute of Behavioral Research, Texas Christian University, 1978.

Johannesson, R. E. "Some Problems in the Measurement of Organizational Climate." *Organizational Behavior and Human Performance*, 1973, *10*, 118–144.

Jordan, P. *A False Spring*. New York: Dodd, Mead, 1975.

Kasarda, J. D. "The Structural Implications of Social Systems Size: A Three-Level Analysis." *American Sociological Review*, 1974, *39*, 19–28.

Katz, D., and Kahn, R. L. *The Social Psychology of Organizations.* New York: Wiley, 1966.

Katzell, R. A., Barrett, R. S., and Parker, T. C. "Job Satisfaction, Job Performance, and Situational Characteristics." *Journal of Applied Psychology,* 1961, *45,* 65–72.

Kendall, L. M. "Canonical Analysis of Job Satisfaction and Behavioral, Personal Background, and Situational Data." Unpublished doctoral dissertation, Cornell University, 1963.

Kenny, D. A. "Cross-Lagged Panel Correlation: A Test for Spuriousness." *Psychological Bulletin,* 1975, *82,* 887–903.

Kerr, W., Koppelmeir, G., and Sullivan, J. "Absenteeism, Turnover, and Morale in the Metals Fabrication Factory." *Occupational Psychology,* 1951, *25,* 50–55.

Kirchner, W. K., and Dunnette, M. D. "Applying the Weighted Application Blank Technique to a Variety of Office Jobs." *Journal of Applied Psychology,* 1957, *41,* 206–208.

Klausner, S. Z. *On Man in His Environment: Social Scientific Foundations for Research and Policy.* San Francisco: Jossey-Bass, 1971.

Kriedt, P., and Gadel, M. "Prediction of Turnover Among Clerical Workers." *Journal of Applied Psychology,* 1953, *37,* 338–340.

Kuhn, T. S. *The Structure of Scientific Revolutions.* (2nd ed.) Chicago: University of Chicago Press, 1970.

LaFollette, W. R., and Sims, H. P. "Is Satisfaction Redundant with Organizational Climate?" *Organizational Behavior and Human Performance,* 1975, *13,* 257–278.

Laughlin, P. R., and Branch, L. G. "Individual Versus Tetradic Performance on a Complementary Task as a Function of Initial Ability Level." *Organizational Behavior and Human Performance,* 1972, *8,* 201–216.

Leavitt, H. J. "Some Effects of Certain Communication Patterns on Group Performance." *Journal of Abnormal and Social Psychology,* 1951, *46,* 38–50.

Lewin, K. *Principles of Topological Psychology.* New York: Harper & Row, 1936.

Lewin, K. *Field Theory in Social Science.* New York: Harper & Row, 1951.

Lcy, R. "Labor Turnover as a Function of Worker Differences,

Work Environment, and Authoritarianism of Foremen." *Journal of Applied Psychology,* 1966, *50,* 497–500.

Lieberman, S. "The Effects of Changes in Sales on the Attitudes of Role Occupants." *Human Relations,* 1956, *9,* 385–402.

Likert, R. *The Human Organization.* New York: McGraw-Hill, 1967.

Lynch, B. P. "An Empirical Assessment of Perrow's Technology Construct." *Administrative Science Quarterly,* 1974, *19,* 338–356.

McCormick, E. J. *Human Factors Engineering.* New York: McGraw-Hill, 1970.

March, J. G., and Olsen, J. P. *Ambiguity and Choice in Organizations.* Drammen, Norway: Harald Lyche, 1976.

March, J. G., and Simon, H. A. *Organizations.* New York: Wiley, 1958.

Minor, F. J. "The Prediction of Turnover of Clerical Employees." *Personnel Psychology,* 1958, *11,* 393–402.

Mischel, W. "Toward a Cognitive Social Learning Reconceptualization of Personality." *Psychological Review,* 1973, *80,* 252–284.

Mobley, W. "Intermediate Linkages in the Relationship Between Job Satisfaction and Employee Turnover." *Journal of Applied Psychology,* 1977, *62,* 137–140.

Mohr, L. B. "Organizational Technology and Organizational Structure." *Administrative Science Quarterly,* 1971, *16,* 444–459.

Morgenstern, O. *On the Accuracy of Economic Observations.* Princeton, N.J.: Princeton University Press, 1963.

Mosel, J. N., and Wade, R. R. "A Weighted Application Blank for Reduction of Turnover in Department Store Sales Clerks." *Personnel Psychology,* 1951, *4,* 177–184.

Overton, W. F., and Reese, H. W. "Models of Development: Methodological Implications." In J. R. Nesselroade and H. W. Reese (Eds.), *Life-Span Development Psychology: Methodological Issues.* New York: Academic Press, 1973.

Palmer, G. L. *Labor Mobility in Six Cities.* New York: Social Science Research Council, 1954.

Parsons, T. *Essays in Sociological Theory: Pure and Applied.* New York: Free Press, 1949.

Perrow, C. *Organizational Analysis: A Sociological View.* Belmont, Calif.: Wadsworth, 1970.

Pervin, L. "Performance and Satisfaction as a Function of Individual Environmental Fit." *Psychological Bulletin,* 1968, *69,* 56–68.

Pfeffer, J., and Salancik, G. R. *The External Control of Organizations: A Resource Dependence Perspective.* New York: Harper & Row, 1978.

Piaget, J. *Biology and Knowledge.* Chicago: University of Chicago Press, 1971.

Porter, L. W., and Lawler, E. E. "Properties of Organizational Structure in Relation to Job Attitudes and Job Behavior." *Psychological Bulletin,* 1965, *64,* 23–51.

Porter, L. W., and Steers, R. M. "Organizational Work and Personal Factors in Employee Turnover and Absenteeism." *Psychological Bulletin,* 1973, *80* (2), 151–176.

Pritchard, R. D., and Karasick, B. W. "The Effects of Organizational Climate on Managerial Job Performance and Job Satisfaction." *Organizational Behavior and Human Performance,* 1973, *9,* 126–146.

Pugh, D. S., and others. "Dimensions of Organizational Structure." *Administrative Science Quarterly,* 1968a, *13,* 65–105.

Pugh, D. S., and others. "Dimensions of Organizational Structure." *Administrative Science Quarterly,* 1968b, *14,* 91–114.

Roberts, K. H., and O'Reilly, C. A. "Organizations as Communication Structures: An Empirical Approach." *Human Communication Research,* in press a.

Roberts, K. H., and O'Reilly, C. A. "Some Correlates of Communications Roles in Organizations." *Academy of Management Journal,* in press b.

Roberts, K. H., and others. "Organizational Theory and Organizational Communications: A Communication Failure? *Human Relations,* 1974, *27,* 501–524.

Robinson, D. D. "Prediction of Clerical Turnover in Banks by Means of a Weighted Application Blank." *Journal of Applied Psychology,* 1972, *56,* 282.

Robinson, W. S. "Ecological Correlations and the Behavior of Individuals." *American Sociological Review,* 1950, *15,* 351–357.

Schmidt, S. M., and Kochan, T. A. "Interorganizational Relationships: Patterns and Motivations." *Administrative Science Quarterly,* 1977, *22,* 220–234.

Schneider, B. "Organizational Climates: An Essay." *Personnel Psychology,* 1975, *28,* 447–479.

Schwab, D. P., and Oliver, R. L. "Predicting Tenure with Biographical Data: Exhuming Buried Evidence." *Personnel Psychology,* 1974, *27,* 125–128.

Scott, W. R. "Organizational Structure." In A. Inkeles (Ed.), *Annual Review of Sociology.* Palo Alto, Calif.: Annual Reviews, 1975.

Seashore, S. E. *Group Cohesiveness as a Factor in Industrial Morale and Productivity.* Ann Arbor: Institute for Social Research, University of Michigan, 1954.

Shaw, M. E. "An Overview of Small Group Behavior." In B. M. Staw (Ed.), *Psychological Foundations of Organizational Behavior.* Santa Monica, Calif.: Goodyear, 1977.

Simon, H. A. *The Science of the Artificial.* Cambridge, Mass.: M.I.T. Press, 1969.

Skinner, B. F. *The Behavior of Organisms: An Experimental Analysis.* New York: Appleton-Century-Crofts, 1938.

Smith, F. J. "Work Attitudes as Predictors of Attendance on a Specific Day." *Journal of Applied Psychology,* 1977, *62* (1), 16–20.

Smith, P. C., and Kendall, L. M. "Retranslation of Expectations: An Approach to the Construction of Unambiguous Anchors for Rating Scales." *Journal of Applied Psychology,* 1963, *47,* 149–155.

Stanfield, G G. "Technology and Organizational Structure as Theoretical Categories." *Administrative Science Quarterly,* 1976, *21,* 489–493.

Stern, G. G., Stein, M. I., and Bloom, B. S. *Methods of Personality Assessment.* New York: Free Press, 1956.

Sutton, H., and Porter, L. W. "A Study of the Grapevine in a Governmental Organization." *Personnel Psychology,* 1968, *21,* 223–230.

Swain, A. D. "Design of Industrial Jobs a Worker Can and Will Do." *Human Factors,* 1973, *15,* 129–136.

Szent-Gyorgi, A. "Dionysians and Apollonians." *Science,* 1972, *176,* 966.

Thompson, J. D. *Organizations in Action: Social Science Bases of Administrative Theory.* New York: McGraw-Hill, 1967.

Torgerson, W. S. *Theory and Methods of Scaling.* New York: Wiley, 1958.

Turner, A., and Lawrence, P. *Industrial Jobs and the Worker.* Cambridge, Mass.: Harvard University Press, 1965.

Udy, S. H. "Administrative Rationality, Social Setting, and Organizational Development." *American Journal of Sociology,* 1962, *68,* 299–308.

U.S. Bureau of Census. *Enterprise Statistics: 1967, P. I: General Report on Industrial Organization.* Washington, D.C.: U.S. Government Printing Office, 1972.

U.S. Office of Strategic Services Assessment Staff. *Assessment of Men: Selection of Personnel for the Office of Strategic Service.* New York: Holt, Rinehart and Winston, 1948.

Wahl, O. F. "Monozygotic Twins Discordant for Schizophrenia: A Review." *Psychological Bulletin,* 1976, *83,* 91–106.

Watson, J. D. *The Double Helix.* New York: Signet, 1968.

Weick, K. E. "Educational Organizations as Loosely Coupled Systems." *Administrative Science Quarterly,* 1976, *21,* 1–19.

Weick, K. E. "Re-Punctuating the Problem." In P. S. Goodman, J. M. Pennings, and Associates (Eds.), *New Perspectives on Organizational Effectiveness.* San Francisco: Jossey-Bass, 1977.

Wiggins, J. S. *Personality and Prediction: Principles of Personality Assessment.* Reading, Mass.: Addison-Wesley, 1973.

Wigner, E. P. "Events, Laws of Nature, and Invariance Principles." *Science,* 1964, *145,* 995–999.

Woodward, J. *Management and Technology.* London: H. M. Stationery Office, 1958.

Woodward, J. *Industrial Organization: Theory and Practice.* London: Oxford University Press, 1965.

Woytinsky, W. S. *Three Aspects of Labor Dynamics.* Washington, D.C.: Social Science Research Council, 1942.

Zadeh, L. A. "Probability Measures of Fuzzy Events." *Mathematical Analysis and Applications,* 1968, *23,* 421–427.

Zadeh, L. A. "A Fuzzy Set Theoretic Interpretation of Linguistic Hedges." *Journal of Cybernetics,* 1972, *2,* 4–34.

Zadeh, L. A. "PRUF—A Meaning Representation Language for Natural Languages." Memorandum ERL-M77/61. Berkeley: College of Engineering, University of California, 1977.

Index

✻ ✻ ✻ ✻ ✻ ✻ ✻ ✻ ✻ ✻ ✻ ✻ ✻ ✻ ✻ ✻ ✻ ✻

165